THE SPIRIT AND THE BRIDE:

Woman in the Bible

Karl Hermann Schelkle

Translated
by
Matthew J. O'Connell

The Liturgical Press

Collegeville   Minnesota

Library of Congress Cataloging in Publication Data

Schelkle, Karl Hermann.
    The spirit and the bride.
    Translation of *Der Geist und die Braut*.
    Includes bibliographical references.
    1. Women in the Bible.   2. Woman (Theology)—Biblical
teaching.   3. Marriage—Biblical teaching.   I. Title.
BS575.S3413   261.8'34'12   79-16976
ISBN 0-8146-1008-0

Nihil obstat: Robert C. Harren, *Censor deputatus. Impri-
matur*: ✠ George H. Speltz, Bishop of St. Cloud, St. Cloud,
Minnesota, April 10, 1979.

    This book was translated from *Der Geist und die Braut*, Patmos
Verlag, Düsseldorf, 1977.

    Printed in the United States of America.

The Spirit and the Bride

Contents

Introduction

The United Nations Organization proclaimed 1975 "International Women's Year." Conferences, news reports, radio programs, and a steady stream of new books continue to discuss the rights and equality of women. All these manifestations are proof that women have in fact not yet achieved their dignity and rights in our society.

The present book adds one more voice to the discussion of these questions and ideas; its contribution is based on the Old and New Testaments, for the position of women in our world is essentially codetermined by the biblical sources of our religion and culture. Yet the texts in question are from two thousand to three thousand years old, and this very fact tells us that biblical history and teaching are in great measure conditioned and limited by the circumstances, attitude to life, and values of their times. We must therefore make an effort if we are to understand the texts and the tradition they represent. The task is first of all historico-critical, but it requires in addition a rounded interpretation that takes all aspects into consideration, since reflection on this source, which the Church understands to be revelation for us, must also serve present-day theological reflection in the Church.

The purpose and goal of this book is a thorough explanation of the biblical texts. Limits have been set to bibliography and explicit exegetical discussion. Nor will the usual dictionaries and reference works be mentioned, since the use of them is to be taken for granted. Even commentaries will be mentioned only in special instances. It goes without saying that at every point I refer the reader to my *Theology of the New Testament*, 4 vols. (Collegeville, Minn: The Liturgical Press, 1971-78).

Many readers will perhaps think that the present book should have had a section on Mary, the Mother of Jesus. I refer them to my book *Die Mutter des Erlösers* (1967³) and to my *Theology of the New Testament* 2:136-77. Considering the important questions of Mariology that are, in my opinion, still open in Catholic theology and magisterial teaching, I could hardly enter upon a new presentation at this time.[1]

The Spirit and the Bride

I

The Old Testament

In the course of a thousand-year history, the Old Testament and early Judaism had experiences of, and achieved insights into, the life and vocation of woman that have been permanently influential. The essentials are contained in the basic religious assertions about creation and redemption. The relevant insights are expressed in a variety of literary forms: myth, saga, history, short story, love poem, law, and maxim.

§ 1. Creation and Sin (Gen. 1-4)[2]

1. Genesis 2:4b-25

Biblical reflection on the history and vocation of woman begins with the story of creation in the Book of Genesis. The stories in Genesis contain Israelite traditions that already have a long history behind them; in repeating these traditions, the stories also continue the discussion with divergent conceptions of reality. For the other cultures and religions of the Old Testament world also had their myths about the creation of the world and man. The acknowledgment of a creator is a universal human phenomenon and not restricted to biblical and Christian religion.

However, the general idea of a creator was interpreted and transformed by the Bible in the light of Israel's faith. As a result, the biblical story of creation says nothing about how the gods came into existence; it contains no genealogy of the gods, no theogony, but only a cosmogony or story of how the world came to be. The God whom Israel had experienced as rescuer during the exodus from Egypt is finally understood to have been creator from the very beginning. The story of creation is thus a prophetic proclamation regarding the past.[3]

The story of the creation of man and woman in the opening chapters of Genesis has had an incalculably broad and profound influence. From early antiquity to our own day, it has been accepted and passed on in writing and books, instruction and sermons, as well as in works of literature and the pictorial arts.

It is an unchallenged conclusion of Old Testament

exegetical scholarship that chapters 1 and 2 of Genesis combine two accounts that differ in origin, character, and style. The earlier account is Genesis 2:4b-25 (which goes with chapter 3). The cultural context it supposes is that of the Davidic-Solomonic era (Gen. 4:17-26), and it is therefore to be assigned to the tenth/ninth century B.C.. Because God is named "Yahweh" in this account, the writer is called the "Yahwist." A somewhat later writer who contributed certain parts is called the "Elohist," because in these sections God is named "Elohim."

The later account of creation (Gen. 1:1-2:4a) comes out of the priestly tradition. Its chief concern is with doctrine, and it represents the result of thinking that is guided by theological principles (for example, in the account of the six days in Gen. 1). The priestly document probably took shape and written form in the sixth/fifth century B.C.. The accounts of the Yahwist, the Elohist, and the priestly document were combined in a redaction that is to be dated in the period after the Babylonian Exile (in the fifth century B.C.).

Individual motifs as well as longer narratives in the creation story are "etiological" stories as far as their literary genre and form are concerned. That is, they are stories intended to show the *aition*, or cause, of the things and situations with which man finds himself involved (for example, the wretched state of the snake, Gen. 3:14-15), then of the situation in which he finds himself, and, ultimately, of the evil state of the world, which is explained in terms of sin and punishment (Gen. 3:16-21).

The interpretation of such passages must endeavor

to bring out the etiological meaning and content of the story. It is quite dubious whether the biblical account permits, and whether it is consistent with its meaning, to reconstruct a happy state that supposedly existed prior to the fall, although dogmatic exegesis endeavors to do just that. This latter kind of exegesis, for example, comes to the conclusion (with Martin Luther) that before the fall the snake resembled a proud rooster. But it would be a mistake to take these etiological stories as reports of historical events and to attempt to prove their historicity, as apologists have rather often tried to do.

The Yahwist story of creation depicts the making of man in well-known words: "Then the Lord God formed man of dust from the ground and breathed into his nostrils the breath of life; and man became a living being" (Gen. 2:7). Non-biblical creation stories likewise tell of the creator-god forming man from mud or clay and breathing life into him.[4]

According to the Yahwist story, the body of man was taken from the dust of the earth and is to decompose into dust again (Gen. 3:19). The power that gives life to man is a divine breath, a divine power. Man possesses life because, and as long as, he breathes. He can expel this breath through his nose. God also forms the animals and creates their life (Gen. 2:19), but of man alone is it said that his life was breathed into him directly by God. Man is raised up above all other living things into the realm of God and into a nearness to God. This special place of man is expressed in the priestly account of creation by saying that man is created according to the image of God (Gen. 1:26-27).

The account of man's creation is meant to explain both the corruptibility of the body and the breath of life. Human life is, however, a bodily thing. Life dies in death. "When thou takest away their breath, they die and return to their dust" (Ps. 104:29). The Greek translation of the Old Testament used "soul" for the Hebrew word meaning "breath of life." According to Greek and especially Platonic philosophy, man has an immortal soul dwelling in his body. When the Christian catechism states that man is composed of a mortal body and an immortal soul, it is transmitting Greek philosophy.

God planted a garden (Greek translation: "paradise") for man in Eden (Gen. 2:8), a garden made fruitful by its abundant waters (Gen. 2:10). Man was to till it and keep it (Gen. 2:15), that is, protect it from harm. This notion corresponds to the much more general commission given to man in the other creation story, that he is to subdue the earth to himself (Gen. 1:28). Man in this garden of God had a commission to fulfill. His life was therefore not simply one of "paradisal" happiness. Rather, work was from the beginning a part of the order and full range of human life.

The biblical story of the creation of the human race has two parts that must be understood as forming a unity; this is especially clear in the Yahwist's account. The man is created first, then the woman. Both are created with a community in view, and it is as members of such a community that God wills their existence. Gen. 2:21-24 makes this clear in the story of the creation of woman. Here again the writer is passing on ancient traditions of his own people and of other people as well who knew of a creation of woman subsequent to the creation of man. Nonetheless, the Yahwist wrote an immortal story about the creation of the human race.

> The account in Gen. 2 reflects a stage of culture at which it was known how important woman is for the humanity of man. Among the myths of the creation of mankind that are found throughout the entire Near East, Gen. 2 is unique in thus setting such a high value on the importance of woman and on the human state as a union of man and woman. . . . It is significant that in our own culture we agree in essentials with what Gen. 2 says of the relation of man and woman.[5]

The divine purpose in creating woman is stated beforehand: "It is not good that man should be alone. I will make him a helper fit for him" (Gen. 2:18). Man and woman are united for mutual help and love. A caring God gives human beings the help and consolation of a community. Woman is not subordinated to man, but coordinated with him in a sharing of life and work.

"And the rib the Lord God had taken from the man he made into a woman" (Gen. 2:22). The story is a puzzling one for us, and the exegetes have given no unanimously accepted explanation of it. It is certain, however, that the account is not to be taken simply as a report of a historical event. At the same time, we are not in a position to say what the tradition was that the writer had inherited and how he revised and interpreted it. A deep sleep falls on the man while God takes a rib from his body. Does this mean that God's making of the woman was hidden from the man, that it was not given him to see and was beyond his power to grasp? Is the formation of woman from the rib of man meant to make concrete the Hebrew idiom according to which a near relative is described as "my bone and my flesh" (Gen. 29:14; Jg. 9:2; 2 Sam. 5:1; Is. 58:7)?

In any case, if some bone of man is to be used for forming the body of woman, the rib is a good choice. It is a principal bone, since it belongs to the center of man's body, where it surrounds and protects the breast and heart. Or should we keep in mind the play on words in Sumerian, where "rib" means "life" or "body"? Then too, the explanation is perhaps to be sought in an entirely different direction, for in the mythology of the cosmos, rib and moon were related. The moon in its phases embodied for early man the mystery of decay and renewal. In its first and last phases, the sickle shape of the moon may be thought to resemble a rib. Is the rib therefore the symbol of life in the process of becoming? Prehistoric human idols that reflect mythic conceptions have parts of the body in the shape of the moon. The account in Genesis would thus place a sickle in God's hand as he sets out to create; this would make it clear that life is not self-caused and that God is the giver and master of life. The woman is then named *havah* (Eve), which means "mother of all living" (Gen. 3:20; see §1.3).[6]

In two additional sayings, one by the male (Gen. 2:23), the other by the narrator himself (Gen. 2:24), the Yahwist gives a meaning to his own story of the creation of Eve. Like a best man, God brings the woman to the man. With rapturous joy the man acknowledges and greets her as the only living thing that is like himself: "This at last is bone of my bones and flesh of my flooh" (Gen. 2:23). Then he gives the woman a name, just as he had previously given names to the beasts. Since he is *ish* (= man), she is *ishah* (= woman).[7] The almost identical names bring out the full parity of the two and their equality of rights.

In the other saying it is the Yahwist himself, the narrator, who speaks: "Therefore a man leaves his father and mother and cleaves to his wife, and they become one flesh" (Gen. 2:24). The bond of love between man and woman is stronger than the previously existing familial bond between parents and children, and dissolves it. The man and woman become "one flesh." Man and woman have been taken one from the other, and therefore they tend to come together and form one flesh again.

The story gives an etiological explanation of marital union. The point of "one flesh" is not that man and woman express themselves as one flesh in a child; the text is rather speaking quite openly of marital union. However, "flesh" (*basar*) in Hebrew does not mean only the sensible, palpable flesh, but includes the whole human being (Is. 40:5; Ezek. 21:4, 10; Ps. 62:3; Lk. 3:6). In this context, then, "one flesh" signifies the very intimate and indissoluble communion of two people. They become *one* person. Such a union is possible only between *one* man and *one* woman. Here, then, the ideal of monogamy finds expression. That is also how the text is understood in the New Testament (Mk. 10:8-9; 1 Cor. 6:17; Eph. 5:32; see §§5.1; 6.1; 7.2).[8]

In Plato's *Symposium* (189D-191D), Aristophanes recounts a myth with comparable motifs.[9] Since the round sphere is the perfect shape, human beings originally existed as spheres. They were male-female beings with four feet, four hands, and two faces. They also possessed great strength and power, and sought to climb up to the heaven of the gods. In order to weaken them, Zeus determined to divide each human being into halves. With Apollo's help, he formed human beings into the two sexes that they now are. The two halves, however, strive to return to unity again. "It is from this distant epoch, then, that we may date the innate love which human beings feel for one another, the love which restores us to our ancient state by attempting to weld two beings into one and to heal the wounds which humanity suffered."[10]

This correspondence in symbolism and ideas between Israel and Greece is very striking. Was the myth of the separation and union of human beings invented twice, or did it derive in both instances from a common source to which we no longer have access?

2. Genesis 1:1–2:4a

Between the older account of creation in Gen. 2:4b–25 and the later one in Gen. 1:1–2:4a, a very important, almost incalculable development had taken place. The older story is bounded by the garden in Eden (Gen. 2:8), while the later one gazes with awe into the incalculable distances of "the heavens and the earth" (Gen. 1:1). The heavens are described as a firmament with sun, moon, and stars (Gen. 1:8, 14, 17). The earth is divided into dry land and seas (Gen. 1:10). The writer of the priestly document is attempting to embrace the fullness of created things as he enumerates them like the wise men of Egypt who catalogued their knowledge.

In the older account, the time period is limited to that of God's dealings with the first human pair; the later account looks back into the mists of immeasurable antiquity (Gen. 1:1). The writer of this later account has the ability to handle the abstract concepts of light and darkness (Gen. 1:3-4). In the older account, God, in creating man and woman, acts as a man would (Gen. 2:7, 21-22), whereas in the later account his word of command creates by itself (Gen. 1:3-26).

The creation of man is described in Gen. 1:26-27: "God created man in his own image . . . male and female he created them." In the history both of exegesis and of dogmatic theology, ever since the time of the early Fathers of the Church, this text has been given a wide variety of interpretations. Contemporary exegetes have concluded that the text means to say "that the Creator created a creature who is his counterpart, to whom he can speak, and who hears him. . . . The special character of man is seen to reside in his ability to enter into a direct relationship with God."[11] Man and woman are both created directly by God; both are created in God's image. Human beings are also from the very beginning created as two sexes and ordered each to the other. Any deliberate or contrived separation of man and woman must take heed that it does not contradict the will of God the Creator. The communion of man and woman has the same meaning as in Gen. 2:18-24.

In their union, the human pair receive God's blessing: "Be fruitful and multiply, and fill the earth and subdue it" (Gen. 1:28). Man and woman receive the blessing in the same manner. Blessing and the power to be fruitful are promised, with the same words, to the beasts (Gen. 1:22). Generation and birth, which in the world around Israel were understood and celebrated in myths of great power and depth as an emanation from and institution of the gods, were in Israel understood and exercised as the abiding will of its God, the Creator.

Marriage is a commission that goes with the created order; it is a command and a duty that are required if creation is to be fulfilled. This accounts for various rabbinical sayings: "The man who is not concerned to reproduce himself is like a man who forgets his own blood." "The unmarried man is like one who diminishes the image of God."[12]

3. Genesis 3:1-4:1

In the Yahwist story of the temptation, sin, and fate of the first human beings in paradise—a story told with a simplicity and profundity, whether artless or, more probably, deliberate, that have been much admired—the woman plays an impressive part. She allows herself to be seduced by the serpent, takes the forbidden fruit, and also passes some of it along to the man. The eyes of both were then opened (Gen. 3:6-7).

Scholars have devoted a good deal of thought to the interpretation of the serpent in paradise.[13] In the myths of East and West alike, the serpent is an animal that both kills and brings life. Because it sloughs off its old skin, it is a symbol of life being renewed. Its poison, moreover, like all poison, can also be a curative agent. Consequently, the serpent was honored in the fertility cults of Israel's Canaanite neighbors. It was a symbol of fruitfulness.

But since the Old Testament uncompromisingly rejected these pagan cults, it also rejected the cult of the serpent. As a result, the serpent, which comes on the scene as tempter in Gen. 3, represents the ongoing major temptation and imperilment to which Israel was subjected by the Canaanite fertility cults. Are these cults being opposed in the form of the serpent in Genesis? This interpretation has often been proposed, but it is hardly plausible in this restrictive form, since the serpent is also described as a creature of God (Gen. 2:19; 3:1) and cannot therefore be a power totally opposed to God or the symbol of such a power.

In the text of Gen. 3, the serpent is simply there, in paradise, as the agent of temptation and evil. No hint is given about where the serpent comes from. The writer gives no information as to the origin of evil; he does not intend, and indeed is unable, to give such information. Evil is simply a given fact. After their deed, the man and the woman are questioned by God about the reasons for what they did (Gen. 3:9-13), but no question is asked of the serpent. No revelation is given concerning the origin and ground of evil. In Gen. 3 evil takes the form of rebellion against God's salutary care of man. The rebellion is puzzling and inexplicable.

In clear reference to the story of creation, the Book of Wisdom says: "God created man for incorruption . . . but through the devil's envy death entered the world"

(2:23-24). The biblical concept of Satan had been developed in the meantime, and the thought is expressed here that the devil was at work in the serpent in paradise. From now on Jewish exegetes regarded the serpent in paradise as commissioned by the devil (Apocalypse of Moses 16), until finally the serpent came to be viewed as the devil in person (Life of Adam and Eve 16). This concept was taken over into the catecheses of the Church.

In this story of temptation and sin, are women in general being portrayed as easily yielding to temptation and then, once having yielded, causing the fall of man as well? Many exegetes think that Gen. 3 is to be understood in such a manner. But it is very questionable whether the story intends to make such a statement. In the conversation between the woman and the serpent, the human person breaks away from, and rebels against, the loving care and order that God has given him for his well-being. His action continues to have its effects throughout the Yahwist history of early man, and these effects are felt in an increasingly deeper way; man here is man as we now know him. Husband and wife, however, continue to share their lives. Hitherto their communion had been one of mutual help and love (Gen. 2:18, 24); now it is a communion in sin and the evils that follow upon sin, as well as a communion in suffering. The relationship between man and woman can thus take widely differing forms.

God's summons discloses the sin. "Where are you?" (Gen. 3:9). God cares for sinful man, and cares for him precisely as sinner. It is the human beings that must answer God's summons; nothing is said to the serpent Man is and remains the one responsible. The two human beings who have hitherto lived in communion and friendship with God now attempt to hide from him. The communion between husband and wife is likewise destroyed. The husband blames the wife, and she in turn blames the serpent. The knowledge that man has usurped in opposition to God's will now turns against him. Whenever man usurps autonomy, he does so to his own harm. Do the answers of the man and the woman (Gen. 3:12-13) contain muted reproaches against God for having acted as he has? "The woman whom thou gavest to be with me ..." (Gen. 3:12); "the serpent," who is called God's creature in Gen. 3:1, "beguiled me" (Gen. 3:13). Is this the beginning of the wrangling and disputing with God that are to be heard going on in Israel and indeed throughout the created world generally?

The three sentences passed on the serpent, the man, and the woman (Gen. 3:14-19) are evidently etiological in their intent. They are meant to explain the situation in which each of the three now lives. The serpent is the only animal that cannot raise itself from the ground; it must live a wretched life in, and apparently by means of, the dust of the earth. To man the serpent is a sinister animal, and the two live in mutual hostility. When the relationship between God and man is disturbed, all of man's other relationships are also disturbed.

As we saw earlier, work was something man was commissioned to do even in paradise. But in the garden of Eden, with its fruitful trees and abundant water (Gen. 2:15), man's work was effortlessly successful.

Now he must laboriously till an unfruitful soil and earn his livelihood as an agricultural worker (Gen. 3:17-19) or a nomad (Gen. 3:18). No matter how hard he works, man cannot change his situation. Only death will put an end to it. But the threatened punishment of Gen. 2:17, the punishment of death, is not actually inflicted. This fact probably indicates a suture in the story. Neither is mortality, for example, inflicted as a punishment, for nowhere previously had man been promised immortality; he had simply been created as a mortal being. The sentences passed by God look rather to man's life as long as it lasts: his life is now a life filled with difficulties.

The life of the woman is characterized by pregnancy and motherhood, which fill a life weighed down by hardship and pain. Her relation to her husband is no longer one of equality (as in Gen. 1:27; 2:18). The wife is now subject to her husband as to a master, and the woman even submits to and desires this humiliating relationship (Gen. 3:16). The Yahwist is thus saying that the subordination of woman to man, which in his time and world was taken for granted, is in fact a corruption of an original ideal state in which man and woman possessed equal rights. The present state of affairs is due to human sin.

Admittedly, the story emphasizes the fact that "the man called his wife's name *havah* (Eve), because she was the mother of all living" (Gen. 3:20). This explanation of the word *havah* (from *hajah*, "life") is the most simplistic kind of etymologizing. What the word *havah* originally meant is in fact unknown. The words in Gen. 3:20 express an undiminished high esteem of woman and motherhood, in contradistinction to the sentence passed in Gen. 3:16. Gen. 3:20 may therefore have been inserted here (by the Yahwist? the later editor?) from another tradition. In any event, despite all else that is said, the text still voices gratitude, joy, and esteem for motherhood.

The high value set upon sexuality and motherhood also finds expression in Gen. 4:1: "Now Adam knew Eve his wife, and she conceived and bore Cain, saying, 'I have gotten a man with the help of the Lord.'" As frequently in the Old Testament (Gen. 17:25; Num. 31:18, 25; Jg. 21:12), sexual union is described as "knowing." In this most intimate of encounters, man experiences the person and value of his partner, and is thus rendered happy. Here too, as in Gen. 2:24, the personal depth of marital union emerges. The mother greets her child as "Cain," a name that perhaps means "a formed being." The mother glories that she has brought forth a man-child. The Old Testament speaks over and over again of the joy of motherhood after the pains of birth (Ps. 113:9; 1 Sam. 2:1-10; see §8).

4. Reservations and Rejection

Man's realization that he is naked is mentioned repeatedly in the biblical story of creation. "And the man and his wife were both naked, and were not ashamed" (Gen. 2:25). "Then the eyes of both were opened, and they knew that they were naked; and they sewed fig leaves together and made themselves aprons" (Gen. 3:7). "I was afraid, because I was naked" (Gen. 3:10). "And the Lord God made for Adam and his wife garments of skins, and clothed them" (Gen.

3:21). Perhaps the reflections expressed in these verses should likewise be regarded as etiological. Did some inkling persist that man had once gone without clothes? Did clothes need to be explained? The crescendo (naked—aprons of fig leaves—garments of skin) sounds like a cultural history of clothing.

It is evident, moreover, that the puzzling phenomenon of shame is being explained. According to the intention of the text, there was originally an utter ease with, and joy in, the body. This self-confident chastity has now been lost. The relation of the human being to his or her body has been disturbed and broken by sin. Man and woman feel shame in each other's presence and not simply before God. Here is the beginning of those reservations with regard to the bodily manifestations of sexuality that find repeated expression in the Old Testament (Ex. 19:15; 20:26; 28:42; Lev. 15:18; 1 Sam. 21:5-6; Ezek. 44:18).

Let us look at some especially striking texts. Before the manifestation of God on Sinai, Moses bids the people keep themselves pure. "And they washed their garments. And he said to the people, 'Be ready by the third day; do not go near a woman' " (Ex. 19:14-15). As the insertion of the words "and he said" shows, verse 15 is clearly a later addition. The purity required in verse 14 is here concretized by identifying it with the purity of sexual continence. Especially is it required that "the priests who come near to the Lord consecrate themselves, lest the Lord break out upon them" (Ex. 19:22).

A comparable development is probably to be seen within the laws of purity in the Book of Leviticus.

It is likely that originally "not a word is said against sexual intercourse" (K. Elliger) in Lev. 15, which contains regulations about sexual discharges. Both in style and in content, Lev. 15:18 is to be regarded as a later addition: "If a man lies with a woman . . .both of them shall bathe themselves in water, and be unclean until the evening."[14]

1 Sam. 21:2-8 narrates the stay of David and his soldiers, who are in flight, with Abimelech, the priest at Nob. David asks for food. The priest has nothing to offer him but the showbread. A condition for eating this is: "if only the young men have kept themselves from women." David answers: "Of a truth women have been kept from us as always when I go on an expedition." Hereupon the priest gives him the showbread. Marital union makes a person cultically unclean. (It is not clear whether David is also saying that the soldiers were obliged to sexual continence by the laws of the holy war.)

The people in the Old Testament had absorbed widespread ideas according to which marital intercourse rendered man and woman unclean (taboo). The unclean person had to avoid association with others until he had purified himself with water. The reason for this view was probably the conviction and fear that nuptials and marital intercourse were especially subject to the threat of demonic attack. In the exercise of sex, the human person was no longer fully in control of himself; he seemed to be in the grip of demonic powers, to be possessed. Those who were thus subject to demons were a danger to other people and had to stay away from them.

This was also why sexual purity and continence were required of an army in the field. This is probably how the words of Uriah, who has come home from battle, are to be understood: "The ark and Israel and Judah dwell in booths; and my lord Joab and the servants of my lord are camping in the open field; shall I then go to my house, to eat and to drink, and to lie with my wife?" (2 Sam. 11:11). Pollution excluded the warrior from the camp (Dt. 23:11-12). Newly wedded men were therefore excused or even excluded from military service (Dt. 20:7; 24:5; 1 Macc. 3:56). This regulation was admittedly interpreted in a more humanistic way later on: the engaged man and the newly married man were to be free to devote themselves to their families for a year, "to be happy with his wife whom he has taken" (Dt. 24:5; see §2.4).

These ideas continued to be influential in the Church. Ex. 19:15 and 1 Sam. 21:5 were invoked to require sexual continence in special cases. Origen exhorts married people to refrain from sexual intercourse for a time before prayer, in accordance with Ex. 19:15 and 1 Sam. 21:5.[15]

Jerome, appealing to 1 Sam. 21:5-6, expects a bishop, who daily offers sacrifice to God, to be especially chaste and pure.[16] In his attack on Jovinian, he invokes 1 Sam. 21:5-6 and explains that marital union makes one unclean.[17] He draws the same conclusion in his homily on Exodus and in his letter to Pammachius.[18] Later on, Augustine of Canterbury likewise invokes 1 Sam. 21:5 in order to require purity for participation in the liturgy.[19]

The Roman Catechism that was issued by the

Council of Trent says with regard to the Eucharist: "The dignity of so great a Sacrament also demands that married persons abstain from the marriage debt for some days previous to communion. This observance is recommended by the example of David who, when about to receive the show-bread from the hands of the priest, declared that he and his servants had been *clean from women for three days.*"[20]

Finally, in his encyclical on holy virginity, Pope Pius XII wrote: "For, if even the priests of the Old Testament had to abstain from the use of marriage during the period of their service in the Temple, for fear of being declared impure by the Law just as other men (see Lev. 15:16-17; 1 Sam. 21:5-7), is it not much more fitting that the ministers of Jesus Christ, who offer every day the Eucharistic Sacrifice, possess perfect chastity?"[21]

The Greek outlook managed to achieve freedom from such conceptions as these (see §4).

5. Eve

This story of sin and punishment in Gen. 3 seems to have been forgotten for centuries in Israel. It was not mentioned in either the Law or the prophets. Only in early Jewish thought of the intertestamental period was attention paid to it again, but now the harsh side of it became predominant. The theologians spoke of Adam's fateful heritage of death and sin. Initially the sin of Adam was the focus of attention (4 Esdras 7:11, 18; Syriac Apocalypse of Baruch 54, 15), less so that of Eve. But gradually more and more emphasis was put on the latter. In a lament about wicked women (Sir. 25:12-25), Jesus, son of Sirach, writes: "From a woman sin had its beginning, and because of her we all die" (25:24).

Jewish theology spoke of the sin committed by both Adam and Eve (Syriac Apocalypse of Baruch 41, 1-2), but Eve was especially blamed. In the Jewish view, Adam was extolled as the perfect, majestic, ideal king, who as such could not be led astray; temptation had to come through Eve. In early Jewish writings, Eve herself is portrayed as giving a detailed description of her temptation by the serpent, admitting her guilt with violent self-reproaches, and lamenting and weeping at her folly (Apocalypse of Moses 19-21; Life of Adam and Eve 17, 2; 26, 2). Adam accuses Eve (Apocalypse of Moses 14). According to Slavonic Enoch (30, 18), in forming Eve from Adam's rib God intended "that death should come to him through his wife." In Philo's allegorical interpretation, Eve becomes the principle of all evil.[22] "For in us mind corresponds to man, the senses to woman, and pleasure encounters and holds parley with the senses first, and through them cheats with her quackeries the sovereign mind itself."[23] Only through the woman could Adam fall.

Paul took over from early Judaism its attention to, and interpretation of, Gen. 1-3 (see §6.1-3).

§ 2. Woman and Marriage in Israel[24]

1. Period of the Patriarchs
(Marriage and Plural Marriage)

The ideal of marriage as presented in the creation story was not fulfilled in Israel. Other conceptions of marriage, especially legal conceptions, are at work in the stories of the patriarchs, which were composed at the same period as the Yahwist story of creation.[25]

Lamech, a descendant of Cain, is the first of whom it is said that he took two wives. It is intimated, probably as a judgment of the Yahwist narrator, that this action was an arbitrary violation of right order (Gen. 4:19-24).

In accordance with a way of acting that the Code of Hammurabi also acknowledges, the hitherto childless Sarah gives her slave Hagar to Abraham as a secondary wife (various traditions are represented in Gen. 16 and 21:9-21). Sarah's spitefulness drives proud Hagar away when she becomes a mother, and Abraham stands helplessly by. The fate of Hagar and her child is depicted with compassion. All the parties concerned get entangled in sin, ultimately the sin of disbelief in God's promise. The "God of vision" looks out for Hagar (Gen. 16:1). Against all expectation he makes Sarah, too, fruitful (Gen. 17:16). As a result, she stands at Abraham's side as "Princess" (Gen. 17:15).

In the story of Isaac's courtship, Rebekah is a charming and lovable fiancée who herself makes the decision to follow Isaac as his wife (Gen. 24:58). At Isaac's prayer, God makes her a mother (Gen. 25:21). But in the struggle between her sons Esau and Jacob,

Rebekah is the biased mother who does not shrink from trickery to gain the advantage for Jacob, her favorite (Gen. 25:28; 27:5-17). Esau marries several foreign women (Gen. 26:34-35; 27:46; 35:1-14), while Jacob marries the two sisters Leah and Rachel (Gen. 29:16-30), and in addition takes their slaves as secondary wives (Gen. 30).

2. Marriage as a Legal Relationship

2.1. Decalogue and Further Regulations

In the Ten Commandments, which may contain words of Moses himself but were only later on developed into their finished form (Ex. 20:1-17; Dt. 5: 6-21), this strict commandment occurs in both versions: "You shall not commit adultery" (Ex. 20:14; Dt. 5:18).[26] Marriage is a state of legal possession. The husband commits adultery when he violates another marriage but not when he has intercourse with, for example, an unmarried girl or a prisoner of war or a slave. The wife commits adultery when she violates her own marriage by intercourse with another man. The man can violate only another's marriage, the woman can violate only her own.

Both versions of the Ten Commandments also forbid coveting the house and wife of one's neighbor; "coveting" probably means plotting to acquire these for oneself (Ex. 20:17; Dt. 5:21). This commandment of the Decalogue is probably a later addition, for it shows a developed morality and casuistry. No longer is it only obvious sins of action that are forbidden, but also sins of thought that lead to sins of action. The commandment in Ex. 20·17 reads: "You shall not covet your neighbor's house; you shall not covet your neighbor's wife." Dt. 5:21, on the other hand, reads: "Neither shall you covet your neighbor's wife; and you shall not desire your neighbor's house, his field. . . ." According to Ex. 20:17, the wife is a part of the house and property of the husband. According to Dt. 5:21, she is no longer simply a part of the husband's property; she is named before the possessions, she is not a thing but a person.

The law allowed no unchastity of any kind whatever in Israel. This sin is an abomination that makes the land unclean and must therefore be eradicated by the death penalty (Lev. 18:28-30). This applies first of all to adultery; both of the guilty parties must be punished by death (Lev. 20:10; Dt. 22:22). The clan must be kept free of incest, and therefore the forbidden degrees of kinship are set down in exact detail (Lev. 18:6-18; 20:11-21). Also forbidden is homosexual intercourse by man or woman, as well as intercourse with animals (Lev. 18:22-23; 20:13, 15-16).

Through marriage the husband becomes the master and possessor (*baal*) of his wife (Gen. 20:3; Ex. 21:22; 24:4; 2 Sam. 11:26; Jl. 1:8; Prov. 12:4; 31:11). The married woman is "taken into possession" (Gen. 20:3; Dt. 21:13; 22:22; Sir. 9:9). The wife addresses her husband as "master" (Gen. 18:12; Jg. 19:26; Am. 4:1; 1 Pet. 3:6), just as the slave does his owner or the subject his king. The burden the word implies was truly felt as a burden, as is made clear in Hos. 2:16, where it is said, with reference to the marital love between Yahweh and Israel: "And in that day, says the Lord, you will call me, 'My husband,' and no longer will you call me, 'My Baal.' "

At times, though not with real frequency, there is reference to a price to be paid for a bride; this is given to the bride and remains hers (Gen. 34:12; Ex. 22: 16-17). Jacob works seven years each for Leah and Rachel (Gen. 29:27). At times, special feats are required, such as Saul requires for the hand of his daughter (1 Sam. 17:25; 18:25). The primitive form of bride-buying was not practiced in Israel.

2.2. *Divorce*

Since the husband was the possessor of the wife, it was possible for him at any time to free himself from her by divorce.[27] In earlier times he probably just sent her away, as Abraham did his secondary wife, Hagar (Gen. 21:14). A formula for this action is perhaps to be inferred from Hos. 2:2: "She is not my wife, and I am not her husband." The right of divorce is handled in Dt. 24:1-4. Here, however, the right is not established but presupposed as already existing; it is now fixed in writing and probably modified as well.

The wife, on the contrary, is a possession of her husband. He can dismiss her, but she has no power to dissolve a marriage. For her protection, however, a legal form is prescribed. The husband must write a bill of divorce and hand it to his wife so that she can prove her freedom. The husband must assert "some indecency" that he has found in his wife. What kind of fault this may be is not stated in the law and was therefore known to all at that period. The fault could not be adultery, however, since this was to be punished by death (Lev. 20:10; Dt. 22:22). Dt. 24:4 prohibits a man who has dismissed his wife from marrying her again. The wife is to be protected against the arbitrary whim of the husband. Here, as so often, the Deuteronomic law manifests its humane attitude.

The interpreters of the law acknowledged, with some hesitation, the woman's right to ask her husband for release when, for example, an illness of the husband or his dishonorable occupation and his acquaintances or her degradation by him made cohabitation with him intolerable.[28]

The rabbis carried on a theological and legal discussion about what Dt. 24:1 meant by the words "some indecency." The school of Rabbi Shammai understood them to mean the wife's infidelity, whereas the school of Rabbi Hillel took them to mean anything at all, including her burning of the food. A man might dismiss his wife if another woman pleased him more, for it says in Dt. 24:1: "if she finds no favor in his eyes." The legal formalities for divorce and the bill of divorce were prescribed in detail."[29] It is this situation that Jesus sharply criticizes in Mt. 19:3 and Mk. 10:2.

Further regulations protected the marriage and the wife's right. The husband was in principle allowed to have more than one wife at a time (Dt. 21:15; 22:19; 1 Sam. 1:2, 6). In addition, he was free to have intercourse with slave-women and female prisoners of war. But he was not allowed to indulge in every whim. A father could sell his daughter (Ex. 21:7), but a husband could not sell his wife (Ex. 21:18; Dt. 21:14). If a man had two wives, he could not neglect either of them, nor could he neglect the children of the wife he loved less (Dt. 21:15-17). If he seduced a virgin, he had to pay the bride-price and take her for his lifelong wife (Ex. 22:16; Dt. 22:28-29). He was not allowed to do as he liked with a slave-woman with whom he had entered into a union. He could not sell her to another, and if he curtailed her marital rights, she went free (Ex. 21:7-11). Similarly, a female prisoner of war gained her freedom if she was dismissed from marriage (Dt. 21:14).

Gideon "had many wives" (Jg. 8:30). The Israelite kings—David (1 Sam. 32:2-3; 2 Sam. 5:13-15), Solomon (1 Kg. 11:1-3; Song 6:8), Rehoboam (2 Chr. 11:21), Abijah (2 Chr. 13:21)—had a harem with numerous wives, thus proclaiming their magnificence and power after the fashion of Oriental kings generally. David's adultery with Bathsheba, wife of Uriah, was condemned without pity, however (2 Sam. 11-12). Solomon's lack of moderation was sharply condemned in 1 Kg. 11:4-8 as well as in later times (Sir. 47:19-20; Neh. 13:26). The law for kings in Dt. 17:14-20, which was probably written at the end of the royal period, says: "He [the king] shall not multiply wives for himself, lest his heart turn away" (17:17). This may have been written with Solomon in mind, since he allowed his pagan wives to lead him into idolatry.

King Herod I (73-4 B.C.) had ten wives, some of them simultaneously. Flavius Josephus criticizes him for this but must admit that "the practice of having several wives at once is possible because of the way the ancestors acted."[30] In New Testament times monogamy was by far the usual practice in Israel, but it was accompanied by the practice of successive marriages after divorce. The property laws played no little part in causing this situation.

3. The Child as Blessing on Marriage

In Israel, children, while not the sole, were certainly the most important meaning and purpose of marriage. In the (priestly) creation story the purpose of marriage is already described thus: "Be fruitful and multiply, and fill the earth" (Gen. 1:28). Barrenness brought a wife to the point of despair; "Give me children, or I shall die," cries Rachel. If a marriage remained childless, the wife might seek to obtain children through secondary wives (Gen. 16:2; 30:3), for she wanted children no matter what, as various stories frankly report (Gen. 19:30-38; 38:12-30). Children were their parents' honor and pride (Ps. 144:12), their joy (Ps. 128:3, 6), and their support (Ps. 127:4-5). Children were a "heritage from the Lord" (Ps. 127:3), a gift from God the Creator. It is the Creator who opens the maternal womb (Gen. 25:21; 30:2). He makes the woman once barren the joyful mother of children (Ps. 113:9). Through the power of Yahweh's promise, the people who had been reduced in numbers while in exile looked for new generations of children (Is. 54:1-3).

So much were children the purpose of marriage that according to the law of marriage with a brother's widow (levirate marriage—a practice that was widespread throughout the ancient East), a brother-in-law had to marry the widow of a brother who had died childless to raise up a posterity for the dead man (Gen. 38:8; Dt. 25:5-6).

4. Marriage as a Love Relationship

The Old Testament is familiar with the idea of marriage as a love relationship. In the (Yahwist) creation story, the man greets the woman with delight when God brings the two together. His nuptial cry of jubilation is the first word spoken between human beings (Gen. 2:23). Even the marriages of the patriarchs, despite their deficiencies, are marked by love. Rebekah was brought to Isaac by a representative who asked for her in marriage. "Then Isaac brought her into the tent, and took Rebekah, and she became his wife; and he loved her. So Isaac was comforted after his mother's death" (Gen. 24:67).

In the story of Jacob and Rachel (Gen. 29:1-30), it is told that "Rachel was beautiful and lovely. Jacob loved Rachel" (vv. 17-18). He spent seven years in service for the sake of Rachel, "and they seemed to him but a few days because of the love he had for her" (v. 20).

Elkanah endeavors to console his childless wife Hannah: "Hannah . . . why is your heart sad? Am I not more to you than ten sons?" (1 Sam. 1:8).

David's marriage to Michal, daughter of Saul, is recorded as part of his story.[31] "Michal loved David." Here, then, the woman chose her husband out of love, and Saul gave her to David as his wife (1 Sam. 18: 20-28). But when Saul became an enemy of David, he married Michal to Palti (1 Sam. 25:44). When David became king after Saul's death, he sent his trusted companion, Abner, and again claimed Michal, who still loved him. Michal was taken from Palti. "But her husband went with her, weeping after her all the way to Bahurim. Then Abner said to him, 'Go, return'; and he returned" (2 Sam. 3:16).

In David's lament over the death of Jonathan, there are these beautiful words about the love of friends and the love of women: "Your love to me was wonderful, passing the love of women" (2 Sam. 1:26).

The oracles of the prophets speak over and over again, in words of great ardor, about a man's first love, the love he has for the chosen wife of his youth (Is. 54: 6; Mal. 2:14–15; Prov. 5:48), and about a woman's love for "the bridegroom of her youth" (Jl. 1:8).

The Preacher, whose thinking is pessimistic in many areas, nonetheless says: "Enjoy life with the wife whom you love, all the days of your vain life which he has given you under the sun" (Eccles. 9:9).

For times of military service and war, Dt. 24:5 prescribes: "When a man is newly married . . . he shall be free at home one year, to be happy with his wife whom he has taken." The original reason for this regulation may have been that weddings and marital communion were regarded as menaced by demons and that the army must be kept free of these (§1.4); but if so, this had long since been forgotten, and the new interpretation shows concern for recent marriages.

After the return from exile, the new order in Israel required the dissolution of marriages that had been contracted between Israelites and foreign women (Ezra 9–10; Neh. 13:23–30). Nonetheless, two men are named who refused this dissolution, and two others agreed with them (Ezra 10:15). For these men, fidelity to wife and marriage was more important than the formal law.

The Old Testament also contains songs of love and marriage. The rejoicing that marks a wedding is the epitome of all festal joy. The prophet must announce that this jubilation will fall silent at the imminent judgment: "And I will make to cease . . . the voice of mirth and the voice of gladness, the voice of the bridegroom and the voice of the bride" (Jer. 7:34; see 16:9; 25:10).

Psalm 45 is an example of a song of love and marriage. The royal bridegroom comes forth in beauty, grace, and victorious power. Equity is his scepter, his throne endures forever in divine splendor. The bride approaches him; she is the daughter of kings and is clad in gorgeous robes and precious jewels. Amid the rejoicing of the people, the procession enters the ivory palace of the king. Their sons will be princes of the earth.

This song may have been written on the occasion of an actual royal wedding or simply for the ideal king. In this second case, the Messiah can be seen in the person of the king. In the New Testament the song is applied to Christ (Heb. 1:8-9). The bride then becomes the messianic community, just as under the old covenant Israel was the wife of Yahweh (Hos. 2:19; §2.5) and in the new covenant the Church is the bride of the Messiah (Eph. 5:25-33; §7.2).

In the Song of Songs, Israel made a lofty contribution to the love poetry of the world, even though the song harks back to foreign and specifically early

Egyptian models. From the second century B.C. on, the Song of Songs was interpreted as an allegory of Yahweh's relationship with Israel; later on, in the Church, it was interpreted as referring to Christ's love for the Church or the soul (and it is still so interpreted by some). But this was not the original meaning. The Song of Songs, which in its essential components probably originated in the early period of Israel's history, bears witness rather to a true and beautiful humanistic outlook. It is not simply popular poetry but already in high degree an artistic creation. It is marked by an ingenuous naturalness, but at the same time by a conscious spirituality. The song describes a passionate, happy, fulfilled love that is lived in a framework of natural beauty.

Precisely in its secularity, however, the songs are an expression of faith. For among the people who were Israel's neighbors, sexuality was understood as being something divine, and it was celebrated as a sacral mystery. In Israel, on the other hand, body and soul were regarded as God's creation and therefore as a gift to man for which he must give thanks. Yahweh himself, however, is neither male nor female and can have no lover.

The portrayal of human beauty in the Song of Songs gives rise to beauty of language. Consider 2:8-14, for example:

> The voice of my beloved!
> Behold, he comes,
> leaping upon the mountains,
> bounding over the hills.
> My beloved is like a gazelle,

or a young stag.
Behold, there he stands
   behind our wall,
gazing in at the windows,
   looking through the lattice.
My beloved speaks and says to me:
"Arise, my love, my fair one,
   and come away;
for lo, the winter is past,
   the rain is over and gone.
The flowers appear on the earth,
   the time of singing has come,
and the voice of the turtledove
   is heard in our land.
The fig tree puts forth its figs,
   and the vines are in blossom;
   they give forth fragrance.
Arise, my love, my fair one,
   and come away.
O my dove, in the clefts of the rock,
   in the covert of the cliff,
let me see your face,
   let me hear your voice,
for your voice is sweet,
   and your face is comely."

In later Old Testament times (ca. 450 B.C.), the prophet Malachi warns his people and censures them because God no longer accepts their sacrifices.

You ask, "Why does he not?" Because the Lord was witness to the covenant between you and the wife of your youth, to whom you have been faithless, though she is your companion and your wife by covenant. Has he not made them (both) to be one (being) of flesh and breath? And what does that one being strive for? Off-

spring from God. . . . I hate divorce, says the Lord (2:
14-16; the text is not entirely certain).

In a few words, the happy experience of new love is
here evoked. God was and remains the witness to it.
This fact calls for fidelity and love. The man who is
faithless to the wife of his youth by dismissing her
"covers his garments with violence" (v. 16). Malachi is
here alluding to the story of creation (cf. Gen. 1:27-28;
2:7, 24), according to which both man and woman
are beings of flesh and spirit who look for children as
God's gift.

We may also mention the non-canonical book
Joseph and Asenath, which acquired its present form
in the second century A.D. but which may contain older
material. The story intends to give the background
for Gen. 41:45, according to which Pharaoh gave
Asenath, the daughter of the chief priest of Om, to
Joseph for his wife.

The purpose of the book is twofold. First of all,
it describes how and why Asenath was won over to
the faith of Joseph and Israel. From this point of view,
the book is part of the missionary literature of Judaism,
which aimed at converting men from belief in pagan
gods to Israel's faith in the one true God. But the book
also uses the techniques of the Hellenistic novel to
depict the love between Joseph and the rich, beautiful,
and highborn Asenath from its beginnings to its fulfillment in marriage. Virginity and self-giving are
portrayed as equally precious. The story is full of
mysterious hints and signs: Joseph possesses messianic
dignity; Asenath receives from God's angel a wonderful meal of bread, wine, and honeycomb that makes

her immortal; Joseph's kiss bestows God's Spirit upon
her; the marriage unites Joseph as God's son to Asenath
as God's bride (Joseph and Asenath 21, 5).

5. Marriage as Image of God's Love

Bridal and marital love were purified and en-
nobled by becoming Israel's image of God's love for
his people.[32] The prophet Hosea was the one who
created image and language in this matter. At God's
command he married a faithless wife. But just as he,
the prophet, still loved his adulterous wife, so God
loves Israel despite her infidelity. God speaks to Israel:
"I will betroth you to me for ever; I will betroth you
to me in righteousness and in justice, in steadfast love
and in mercy. I will betroth you to me in faithfulness,
and you shall know the Lord" (2:19). "When Israel was
a child, I loved him" (11:1).

Later prophets reminded Israel of this as they
accused her of her sins. Thus Isaiah: "How the faithful
city has become a harlot, she that was full of justice!"
(1:21). The certainty of her election continued, however, to be a consolation and a promise in times of
disaster. Jeremiah was still forced to tell the people,
as God's spokesman: "I remember the devotion of
your youth, your love as a bride, how you followed
me in the wilderness" (2:2). Both of the kingdoms,
Israel and Judah, are faithless and rebellious; they have
prostituted themselves to foreign gods. Yet God calls
them back, saying: "I am merciful. . . . I will not be
angry for ever" (3:12; see 3:1-13).

From the beginning, God has made himself known
to Israel, and he now says: "I have loved you with an

everlasting love; therefore I have continued my faithfulness to you" (Jer. 31:3). He does not forever reject the faithless wife by giving her a bill of divorce (Jer. 3:8; Is. 50:1); he remains Israel's husband. "Can a man cast off the wife of his youth? says the Lord" (Is. 54:6). God will again make glorious the one who was rejected (Is. 60:15). "For as a young man marries a virgin, your Builder shall marry you. As a bridegroom rejoices over the bride, so shall your God rejoice over you" (Is. 62:5).

Ezekiel finds himself forced to accuse Israel of infidelity. Both kingdoms, Israel and Judah, are faithless prostitutes (Ezek. 16 and 23), and God will put an end to their lewdness (Ezek. 23:48-49). And yet he is mindful of the covenant he made with Israel in her youth (Ezek. 16:60).

From the second century B.C. on, the Song of Songs was interpreted, with the help of the ancient symbolism, as referring to the love of Yahweh for Israel. — The image of the marital love of God and Christ for the community continues in the New Testament (Mt. 2:19-20; 2 Cor. 11:2; Eph. 5:25-33; Rev. 21:2; 22:17; see §7.2).

6. The Sapiential Literature

In the sapiential literature of the Old Testament, warnings against lewdness and exhortations to marital fidelity constitute an important and frequently recurring theme. Israel's wisdom as a whole reflects a long tradition to be found in Egypt, Sumer, Babylon, and Canaan. Literary collections of proverbs and sayings grew up everywhere and exerted an influence on Israel. The beginnings of her own sapiential tradition may go back as far as Solomon. According to 1 Kg. 4: 32, Solomon composed three thousand proverbs and one thousand and five songs. For this reason, later literary collections were likewise attributed to him (Prov. 1:1: "The proverbs of Solomon . . ."; Wis. 9:7-8). The sapiential literature continues in the Book of Jesus son of Sirach and thus down to the second century B.C. The sayings are often statements of worldly prudence, but they are offered in a religious spirit: "The fear of the Lord is the beginning of knowledge" (Prov. 1:7; 9:10). The Book of Proverbs contains long series of texts that warn the reader against "the alien woman," adultery, and consorting with prostitutes (Prov. 2: 16-19; 5:1-23; 6:20-7:27; 23:27-28).

A (probably late) appendix to the Book of Proverbs contains in its opening verses admonitions given by the mother of Lemuel, king of Massa, an Arabian prince, to her son (31:1-9). Thus the wisdom of foreigners was accepted into the Bible. The mother recommends that her son practice the virtues of frugality, moderation, and justice.

The Book of Proverbs ends with a song in praise of the wife and mistress of the house (Prov. 31:10-31). The twenty-two verses begin with the successive letters of the Hebrew alphabet, an artistic form that was cultivated in the postexilic period and was intended as an aid in remembering the poem for repetition. This song of praise first lauds the fidelity and solicitude of the wife for her husband and children. "The heart of her husband trusts in her." The husband is portrayed as a distinguished and respected judge, who as a member of the council helps administer the city and the land. It is as an independent mistress but also as a cheerful helper that the wife keeps order in the house and increases its possessions. She is solicitous for others: the domestics, the poor, and the needy. "She is respected in the city gates." Dignity, wisdom, and fear of God characterize her. This sublime poem gives a picture of woman that captures both reality and ideal. It is an extraordinary testimony to the esteem in which women were held in postexilic Israel, and to the freedom they enjoyed.

The Book of Tobit (which probably dates from the second century B.C.) forms part of the wisdom literature. Its main subject is the marriage of Tobiah to Sarah, a relative of his. God has from eternity decreed marriage between them (6:18), and he sends his angel to bring them together (12:14-15). For his part, Tobiah "fell in love with her and yearned deeply for her" (6:18). On their wedding night, Tobiah prays: ". . . O God of our fathers. . . . thou madest Adam and gave him Eve his wife as a helper and support. From them the race of mankind has sprung. Thou didst say, 'It is not good that the man should be alone; let us make a helper for him like himself' " (8:5-6). The prayer echoes the story of creation in Gen. 1-2. This was a story Israel loved to recall. For the pious, it was witness to the fact that marriage had been established by God himself. The prayer cites Gen. 2:18 and has echoes of Gen. 1:26 and 1:28. Marriage is here given a spiritual meaning. It is not desire for property nor passion that brings the spouses together, as is shown when Tobiah prays: "I am not taking this sister of mine because of lust, but with sincerity" (8:7).

However, the Book of Tobit also seems to have preserved some very ancient conceptions. Thus, the demon Asmodeus plays a vicious role in the story (3:8; 6:8; 8:3). He has killed seven husbands when they sought to consummate their marriage to Sarah. This is probably an example of the belief that sexual relations were in a special way menaced by demons (§1.4). At one point the text reinterprets the death of the seven: they became sacrificial offerings to the demons because their hearts were evil. The angel explains: "The ones the demon can overcome are those who in marriage banish God from their thoughts and actions and abandon themselves to their instincts" (6:16-17 in the Vulgate text).

The late story of Susanna (Dan. 13) was incorporated into the expanded Old Testament canon. Her name means "lily" and probably refers to her purity and beauty. The story gives an example of the marital fidelity that draws down God's protection, while the wickedness that sets a snare for it pays the penalty of death.

In the Book of Jesus son of Sirach, too, there are many texts relating to right order in marriage and family and to the disruption of this order. Sir. 23: 12-27 is a warning against lewdness; 9:1-9 gives advice for dealing with women; 22:27-23:6 is a prayer for purity in word, thought, and action; 25:1-26:27 portrays the harmonious married life, with 25:1-11 depicting the bad and the good husband, and 25:13-26:27 the bad and the good wife; 36:23-31 extols the happiness of the man whose wife is both beautiful and good. This Book, like the rest of the wisdom literature, has a religious keynote: "All wisdom comes from the Lord and is with him for ever" (1:1).

The supreme values in a wife are morality and piety (Prov. 31:30; Sir. 26:23). Even the barren wife is to be called happy if she is undefiled (Wis. 3:13). Israel is set apart as holy for the Lord and may not stain herself with any impurity (Jubilees 20, 8). In Jewish proverbial wisdom, the wife stands beside her husband as a highly esteemed partner.

7. Above and Beyond the Law

Judaism, though its piety was centered on the law, was not satisfied with legalism and casuistry in dealing with sexuality and marriage, but looked for something more: premarital continence and marital fidelity. The law still allowed more than one marriage at a time, but monogamy was practiced almost without exception. The forceful admonitions of the wisdom literature against unchastity and adultery (Prov. 2: 16-19; 6:20-29; 7:5-27; 30:20; Sir. 9:1-9; 23:14-27; 42: 9-12) show that lapses were not rare, but they also show that in Judaism people did not take these as lightly as among other peoples.

Infidelity is a sin against both man and God. The seductive alien woman "forsakes the companion of her youth and forgets the covenant of her God" (Prov. 2: 16-17). The pious woman prays, "Let neither gluttony nor lust overwhelm me, and do not surrender me to a shameless soul" (Sir. 23:6). In the past history of Israel, Sodom and Gomorrah stand as cautionary examples of punishment for immorality (Gen. 19:1-29; Jer. 23:14; Jubilees 20, 6; 3 Macc. 2, 5; Testament of

Naphtali 3, 4; 4, 1; Mt. 10:16; Jude 7; 2 Pet. 2:6). In the stories of the patriarchs, it is recorded of Jacob's sons Reuben (Gen. 21:22) and Judah (Gen. 38:16) that they yielded to lust. In the Testaments of the Twelve Patriarchs, these two admit their guilt and warn others against this sin (Testament of Reuben 3, 11-15; Testament of Judah 4).

Judaism was aware that its sexual morality, more than anything else, distinguished it from the surrounding pagan world (Letter of Aristeas 152; Jubilees 25, 1; Sibylline Oracles 3, 591-600; 1 Cor. 5:1). Idolatry is the beginning and cause of unchastity (Wis. 14: 12-29; Rom. 1:24-27; 1 Thess. 4:5). In the New Testament period, Philo (*On the Special Laws* III, 7-82) severely condemns the vices of the pagans and calls for strict sexual discipline as he interprets the Decalogue and the law of Lev. 18 on marriage. It is not an accident that he, like the Greek translators of the Old Testament, puts the prohibition of adultery ahead of the prohibition of murder in the Decalogue, and thus places it at the head of the second table. In the judgment of Qumran, Belial snares Israel with three nets: unchastity, riches, and defilement of the sanctuary (Damascus Document 4, 15). In the catalogues of vices in the Qumran scrolls, there are warnings against unchastity (1 QS 4, 10; Damascus Document 4, 20; 7, 1; 8, 5).

The rabbis devoted themselves to detailed interpretation of the law. In their view, whatever the law did not forbid was by no means automatically good and allowed. One rabbi says: "If a man leaves his first wife, the altar sheds tears." In the Old Testament and the later writings, we find statements comparable to

Christ's assertion that the lustful gaze is already an act of adultery (Mt. 5:24). Thus Num. 15:19 and Hos. 6:9 speak of the "unchaste hearts and lustful eyes" that look for idols. The expression recurs in 1 QS 1, 6; 1 QpHab 5, 7; Damascus Document 2, 16. Some other sayings: "I have made a covenant with my eyes; how then could I look upon a virgin?" (Job 31:1). "A wife's harlotry shows in her lustful eyes, and she is known by her eyelids" (Sir. 26:9-11). "His eye looks lustfully on every woman, and his tongue lies in swearing to a marriage compact. With his eyes he makes a sinful agreement with every woman" (Psalms of Solomon 4, 4-5, on the hypocrite in the council). "I did not lift my eyes for illicit love" (Testament of Issachar 7, 2). And the rabbis say: "You shall not commit adultery, either with hand or with eye or in your heart." "Do not say that he alone is an adulterer who violates his marriage with his body; he who does it with his eyes is likewise an adulterer."

Pharisaic Judaism believed that marriage was the natural human state and the one in accord with creation. These are some of the sayings of the rabbis on the point: "The Jew who has no wife is not a man." "The Jew without a wife is a man without joy, blessing, or possessions." "The man who lives without a wife lacks peace." Only in his wife does a man find refreshment for his soul." "There is a substitute for everything but the wife of one's youth." Marriage is taken so much for granted that at the circumcision of a boy the prayer is offered that "as he has entered into the covenant, so may he enter upon the law, under the marriage canopy, and into good works."[33]

8. Questions and Reservations

For earlier times, but especially for the New Testament period, we shall adduce witnesses showing that the judgment passed on women was uncertain and divided. According to Lev. 12:2-3, the uncleanness of a woman lasts for forty days after the birth of a boy, eighty days after the birth of a girl. The uncleanness caused by a girl seems to be greater than that caused by a boy. But the reason is this: When the regulations for purification after birth were originally laid down, the processes of birth, like those of the sexual life generally, were regarded as especially menaced and affected by demons, and, since the female sex was considered especially susceptible to demonic influences (Gen. 3; §2.5), a double period of purification was thought necessary after the birth of a girl.

According to ancient usage, men and women were to have the same rights at religious feasts (§3.2). But another, probably later, prescript says: "Three times in the year shall all your males appear before the Lord God" to celebrate the feasts (Ex. 23:7; Dt. 16:16). The Talmud orders that women not receive instruction, for "the man who teaches his daughter the torah teaches her to be dissolute."[34] A synagogue service could be held only when ten males were present; women were not counted. Women also had to keep silent during services; they could not do the readings or even speak; they could not interpret or teach. Women, slaves, and children were not obliged to say aloud the confession of faith (the *Shema*). When men were present, women could not even say the blessing at meals. It was regarded as "disgraceful" for a woman's voice to be heard in public. A man was not even to speak to a woman in public; "that refers to his own wife; how much more does it apply to the wife of another."

In the synagogue, women were set apart, in the gallery if possible (this is the rule even today in European synagogues). While in the two earlier temples at Jerusalem there were no separate places for men and women, the Herodian Temple, which existed in the New Testament period, had two forecourts for visitors: the "court of Israel" and the "court of women." Women were not acceptable witnesses in court. Women and girls could not even serve table. It was a rabbinical principle that a man was not to let a woman serve him.[35] Rabbi Judah sums it up when he says: "Blessed be God who did not create me a pagan or a woman or an ignoramus" (this saying is attributed to other rabbis as well, but also to Persians and Greeks).

Early Judaism also recognized and practiced continence in marriage.[36] One of the oldest attestations of it is in the Testament of Naphtali: "There is a time for marital intercourse and a time to be continent in order to pray" (8, 8). The rabbis endeavored to make detailed applications of this principle. Thus married persons could oblige themselves to abstinence in marriage for a week at a time, according to one view, or for two weeks, according to another. For the purpose of studying the law, a man was allowed to absent himself from his wife for thirty days or, according to another view, for years at a time, and this even without the consent of his wife.[37] Paul too accepts such restrictions on intercourse (1 Cor. 7:5), but he presupposes the agreement of both spouses (§6.3).

Another reservation is to be found in the Jewish apocalyptic literature. The prophets had already announced that in the distress of the end-time there would be no weddings with their rejoicing (Jer. 7:34; 16:9; 25:10; Bar. 2:23). A constant theme in the apocalyptic descriptions of the coming disaster is that on that day the childless will be called happy. "Betrothed pair, do not enter the bridal chamber! Virgins, lay aside the adornments on your bridal wreath! Wives, ask not for the blessing of children! Rather should the barren be glad" (Syriac Apocalypse of Baruch 10, 13-14). The distressed will carry their children away and forget their nurslings (Ethiopian Enoch 99, 5-6). "The barren and the virgins say: 'We rejoice that we have no children'" (Apocalypse of Elijah 28, 4). Women will cease to bear children (Sibylline Oracles 2, 164-65). Although 6 Esdras may have originated in the Christian period, the admonition in 2(16), 40-45 seems to reflect Jewish traditions as it urges detachment from the world in the manner of 1 Cor. 7:29-30. Verse 45 says: "Let those who are married act as though they begot no children! Let those who are not married act as though they were widowed!"[38] The Apocalypse of St. John uses the same motif in describing the fall of Babylon (= Rome): "The voice of bridegroom and bride shall be heard in thee no more" (18:23). This message becomes very strong in New Testament eschatology (§§5.6; 6.7).

The members of the Qumran community who

lived at Qumran were unmarried.[39] The Rule of the Community (1 QS) says nothing of women and children, but the Rule of the Congregation (1 QSa 1, 4) and the Damascus Document (4, 20-5, 2) do mention them. This probably means that members who were more loosely related to the community and lived in the vicinity could be married. Flavius Josephus, too, reports the same of the Essenes, who were probably identical with the Qumran community. He also gives reasons for the practice of celibacy. He says (Jewish War 2, 121) that the Essenes did not marry because they did not trust a wife to be faithful. In addition, the Essenes regarded marriage as the source of all conflict (Antiquities 18, 21). According to Philo,[40] the Essenes did not marry because women are selfish, jealous, and hypocritical, and turn their husbands into slaves.

Thus understood, celibacy at Qumran would have been an expression of the pessimism about marriage and life generally that arose in late antiquity and has here and there been a sign that a culture is decadent and jaded. But it may be that here again, as on other occasions, Philo and Josephus had their Greek readers in mind and were offering explanations that these readers would understand and find acceptable, but were in fact saying nothing of the real reasons. The true reasons probably emerge more accurately from other contemporary Jewish writings accepted at Qumran.

According to the Damascus Document, marital intercourse was not permitted "in the city of the sanctuary" (which probably means not all of Jerusalem but only the Temple precincts), so as not to "defile the city of the sanctuary with their impurity" (12, 1-2).[41] According to Jubilees 50, 8, "the man who has intercourse with his wife on the sabbath shall die." Marriage was thus felt to cause cultic uncleanness; various Old Testament prescriptions, as in Lev. 15:18, and the story in 1 Sam. 21:5 can be understood in the same way (§1.4). Thus it was perhaps also the fear of ritual uncleanness that determined the narrower Qumran community to practice celibacy. In addition, the Qumran community was filled with an intense eschatological expectation. The devout knew themselves to be the "Israel of the final days" (1 QS 1, 1). Perhaps this expectation was another reason for celibacy, since in the distress of the end-time, marriage could be regarded as a troublesome burden (see above).

§ 3. Women in the Family, the Liturgical Community, and the History of Israel

1. Women in the Family

Order within the family is based on one of the Ten Commandments: "Honor your father and your mother, that your days may be long in the land which the Lord your God gives you" (Ex. 20:12; see Deut. 5:16).[42] This commandment goes far beyond some other commandments of the Decalogue, which prohibit specific serious offenses such as murder, adultery, and theft. This commandment calls for an interior attitude of reverence that never becomes out of date and that must constantly give rise to new actions.

Father and mother are named together without distinction. As among other peoples, so in Israel there may at one time have been a matriarchal type of family, at least in individual nomadic tribes, but if so, it was replaced by the patriarchal family by the time of the establishment of the nation, at the latest. (The basis for a primitive matriarchy is probably the fact that in sexual relations it is certain who the mother is but not who the father is.) In a patriarchy the woman is more easily forced into a weaker position in the family; this is especially so when polygamy is practiced. Yet in the commandment father and mother stand side by side as possessed of equal rights. Both have the same claim to respect and obedience in the family. In fact, Lev. 19:3 even names the mother ahead of the father: "Every one of you shall revere his mother and his father . . . I am the Lord your God." The commandment that parents be honored is highlighted by being grounded in the holy will of God.

The mother-father sequence appears only in Lev. 19:3; 20:19; 21:2. The exegetes endeavor to explain these unusual texts. It is difficult to maintain that the priority of the mother represents an echo of matriarchy. Did a loosening of the kinship and family organization toward the end of the pre-exilic period lead to a special emphasis on respect for parents and especially for the mother (as M. Noth thinks)? Or, at the time when the Book of Leviticus was being edited, was the authority of the mother especially threatened, as

Mal. 2:10-16 seems to indicate (so K. Elliger)?[43]

Even in later texts, father and mother are named together. For example, in Prov. 1:8: "Hear, my son, your father's instruction, and reject not your mother's teaching" (see also Prov. 10:1; 15:20). Prov. 19:26 and 30:11-12 warn against any contempt or mistreatment of father and mother. The children should not seize their inheritance ahead of time (Prov. 28:24).

In the Decalogue, the commandment about honoring parents is placed (deliberately, in all probability) before the other aspects of the social order, and it alone is singled out by the promise "that your days may be long in the land which the Lord your God gives you." The promised land is the sign and guarantee of God's blessing and grace. These are promised to those who reverence their parents. The Book of the Covenant reinforces the commandment of the Decalogue by ordaining the death penalty for anyone who curses or strikes father or mother (Ex. 21:15, 17). The commandment of respect for parents remains a central theme of instruction (Sir. 3:2, 4; 7:27; 23:14; Tb. 4:3-4; Letter of Aristeas 238). The synagogue clarifies the commandment in a number of further rules.[44]

In the New Testament the old order retains its validity, as Jesus reasserts this commandment along with the others of the Decalogue (Mt. 10:19). He requires the true and entire fulfillment of this commandment (Mt. 7:9-13). Accordingly, it too appears in the lists of duties incumbent on the members of the domestic society (the *Haustafeln*: Eph. 6:1-3; Col. 3: 20; §7.1).

2. Women in the Liturgical Community

Not a few peoples in the world around Israel had priestesses. In fact, in Eastern religions a high priestess might even be regarded as the spouse of the god she served. In Babylon there were thirty categories of priests and twenty of priestesses and women serving in the temples. Especially did women function as priestesses in the service of the goddesses, as with Isis in Egypt, Hera in Greece, and Vesta at Rome. In Israel, however, there were never any priestesses of Yahweh.

This does not mean that women were excluded from the religious and liturgical celebrations of early Israel. They took part in the national festivals (Dt. 12: 12; 2 Sam. 6:18). They engaged in liturgical dancing (Ex. 15:20-21; Jg. 21:21) and went in procession with the men (Ps. 68:28). At Shiloh women had access to the temple and shared in the sacrificial meals (1 Sam. 1:4-10). The Passover was originally a feast of the entire family (Ex. 12:3-4), as was the Feast of Weeks (Dt. 16:10-12) and the Feast of Booths (Dt. 16:13-17). According to Dt. 29:10-12, men and women, children and sojourners were to be accepted into the covenant with God. According to Dt. 31:12, the law was to be read every seven years at an assembly of the entire people, to "men, women, and little ones, and the sojourner within your towns, that they may hear and learn to fear the Lord." (Admittedly, this precept was later on given a restrictive application: Ex. 23:17; Dt. 16:16.)

Women ministered at the tent of meeting (Ex. 38:8). Since these women had given their (metal) mirrors for making a laver of bronze, they evidently belonged to the class of well-off people. They are mentioned again in 1 Sam. 2:22, where it is reported that the dissolute sons of Eli had intercourse with them. The scanty references do not enable us to say just what service these women performed.[45] Women, like men, could take the Nazirite vow, and if they did, they were regarded as specially consecrated to God (Num. 6:1–21).

Two hundred and forty-five male and female singers returned to Jerusalem from the Babylonian Exile (Neh. 7:67). After the return, the Temple services, and especially the sacrifices and the liturgy, were carefully reorganized. For Ezra's reading of the law, both men and women assembled (Neh. 8:2), but no further mention is made of women in the celebration of the liturgy. They were excluded from active participation in worship, which was the prerogative of males. The Passover meal became a gathering for men, from which women, children, and slaves were excluded.[46] Early Judaism limited the rights of women even more (§2.8).

In contrast with this development, it is very significant that at various periods of Israel's history we find women acting as prophetesses. In this context it should be noted that prophecy did not originally mean a prediction of future events, but included any proclamation of God's instruction and word. In an early period (about the twelfth century B.C.), Deborah is called a prophetess in Israel. She lived in the time of the "judges," who governed in the period after the migration into Canaan, when there were initially no

kings. These men defended the freedom of the Israelite tribes against the enemies who pressed hard
on them from without, but they also had the task of
assuring justice and order within Israel. Their pre-
eminence among the people was due to divine call
(Jg. 2:16). "The Spirit of the Lord came upon him"
(3:10).

Along with the many men who are mentioned
as judges, Deborah is named with special honor as
a "judge over Israel," and for a long time after, people
used to point out the "palm of Deborah," under which
she sat when giving her judgments (4:4). Justice and
religion were closely connected in Israel; the law was
God's law and holy order. As a judge, Deborah was
also a prophetess, since she pronounced her decrees
in the light of Israel's faith and under the movement
of God's Spirit. She was leader of the people in the
war against the Canaanites, who harassed Israel for
twenty years. She, a woman, communicated the order
for battle to Barak, commander of the army. "The
Lord, the God of Israel, commands you, 'Go, gather
your men at Mount Tabor, taking ten thousand from
the tribe of Naphtali and the tribe of Zebulun.'" Barak
acknowledges the woman's call: "If you will go with
me, I will go; but if you will not go with me, I will not
go" (4:6-9). On the day of decision, Deborah orders
the attack (4:12). After the victory, it is also her privilege to sing the song of triumph (5:1, 12). She is given
the honorary title "mother in Israel" (5:7). She has been
called the "Maid of Orléans" of the Old Testament.

Miriam, the sister of Moses, is likewise called a
prophetess. After the passage of the sea, she led the

women in a triumphal dance and sang the song of victory (Ex. 15:20). Together with Aaron, on one occasion she appealed to the fact that God had spoken to her too and not only to Moses, and the two of them became enraged at Moses when he married a Cushite woman. For this, Miriam was punished with leprosy, but she was healed of it through Moses' intercession (Num. 12:1-15).

In the time of King Josiah (638-608), when the great prophet Jeremiah was active, we read of a prophetess named Huldah at Jerusalem, who was held in high esteem. When the long-lost and disregarded Book of the Law was found, the king sent messengers to ask the prophetess what would happen. She announced the divine sentence, that the king would die in peace but that after his death disaster would come upon the city because of its idolatry (2 Kg. 22:14-20).

Just as there were false prophets in Israel, so also were there false prophetesses. Ezekiel condemns those "daughters of your people, who prophesy out of their own minds" and who by their superstitious words and practices confirm the wicked in their ways and lead the good astray (13:17-22).

There is another mention of a false prophetess in Neh. 6:14. Some of the notables of Jerusalem, "and also the prophetess Noadiah," were planning measures against Nehemiah the governor and against the building of the wall which he had undertaken.

The New Testament tells of a final prophetess in Israel. When the child Jesus was brought to the Temple, the elderly Simeon—"the Holy Spirit was upon him"—proclaimed salvation through the coming of the Messiah and also announced the fate of the Messiah's mother (Lk. 2:25-34). "And there was a prophetess, Anna, daughter of Phanuel," who after seven years of marriage had remained a widow until her present advanced age. She had probably always acted as a prophetess among the people. Now "she gave thanks to God, and spoke of him to all who were looking for the redemption of Israel" (Lk. 2:36-38).

The spirit of prophecy is promised to all in the messianic era. In his sermon on Pentecost, Peter explains that the expectation of a universal giving of the Spirit, in accordance with Jl. 2:28-32, has now been fulfilled (Acts 2:17-21; §11.1). Joel had said that, along with free men, servants and handmaids too would receive the Spirit and become prophets. Peter interprets Joel as saying, "my servants and my maidservants." In other words, the word of God also applies to servants and handmaids in the new people of God. — In the New Testament community, both prophets and prophetesses were active (1 Cor. 11:5; §12.5).

The promise of the Spirit and Spirit-filled speech must be valid always and for all men and women in the Church. It cannot be retracted by such statements as 1 Cor. 14:34 and 1 Tim. 2:11-12, which bid women be silent in the community (§§12.5; 13.1).

3. Women in the History of the Nation

Alongside the patriarchs Abraham, Isaac, and Jacob, their wives stand as tribal ancestresses. Other women, too, played significant roles in the national community.

In the (complete) Old Testament canon, three

books bear the names of women: Ruth, Esther, and Judith. These three books belong to the postexilic period and are evidence of the importance later Judaism attributed to women as it looked back over its history.

The Book of Ruth is a charming short novel. It depicts the lot of two strong, religious women, mother-in-law and daughter-in-law, who experience the protection of a kindly, prudent man. God leads the faithful to alien lands as well as to their homeland, and after suffering he gives happiness. Ruth becomes a tribal ancestress of the Messiah.

The Book of Esther can be described as a historical novel. Its scene is the fabulous, far-off Persian empire. The king chooses Esther, a beautiful Jewess, as his queen, and she, along with her people, is rescued from deadly peril. Here religion and nationality are identified. In fact, strictly religious motifs are lacking entirely, at least in the original form of the book. Many thousands of enemies of the Jews are slain (9:16).

The book is interesting and exciting to us today as an early witness to the persecution of an Israel that had developed into Judaism. We can already hear the accusations that anti-Semitism levels against the Jewish people: "There is a certain people scattered abroad and dispersed among the people in all the provinces of your kingdom; their laws are different from those of every other people, and they do not keep the king's law, so that it is not for the king's profit to tolerate them. If it pleases the king, let it be decreed that they be destroyed" (3:8-9).[47]

Judith is a widow, faithful to her one husband,

beautiful, rich, and devout. The artistically written narrative may be a free invention or may at most contain a historical remembrance of the heroic deed of a Jewish woman who rescued her native city amid the difficulty and stress of war. The story is shot through with religious and national passion. But it is a woman who receives the acclamation: "You are the exaltation of Jerusalem, you are the great glory of Israel, you are great pride of our nation!" (15:9).

Christian criteria are not to be applied to every detail of these writings. We need not decide whether the Church would share the well-known harsh judgment of Martin Luther in his *Table Talk*: "I am so hostile to this book [2 Macc.] and to Esther that I wish they were not there at all. They judaize too much and contain a good deal of pagan duplicity."

II

Woman and Marriage in the New Testament

In the experience of modern society, the task and duty of living married life in as perfect a way as possible is a difficult one. Married couples are no longer supported by the clan or extended family, but then neither are they willing any longer to follow a path prescribed for them by the extended family. The personal intimate union of the partners has become the ideal of marriage. External legal institutional forms are often of little help and may even be felt as a limitation on freedom. When it comes to the concrete ordering of married life, questions arise that are often not easily solved, such as free union versus civil and ecclesiastical legal forms; mixed marriages between persons of different religious confessions; the purposes of marriage and responsible parenthood; frequently, too, the failure and breakup of a marriage.

For such questions as these no answer, or at least no direct answer, is to be gotten from the New Testament. The questions are themselves the result of a long historical development or may even have their basis in the conditions of modern society, conditions that are quite different from those of the New Testament period. Yet it is not only the world in the sense of the society in which we live that has changed; the world that we experience inwardly has also changed. If the problems affecting marriage today are to be clarified and mastered both in education and in pastoral practice, we feel that it is essential for us to understand the relation between marriage and eros, and to interrelate the two as forces that produce, support, and fulfill each other.

It is true, of course, that we have inherited from ages past some profound statements about marriage and marital fidelity. But only since the Romantic period have poetry and philosophy really spoken in a reflective and forceful way about the experience of love and marriage as a fulfillment of the whole person. Only in very recent years, moreover, have a philosophy and ethos of existence and personalism emerged. The New Testament has nothing to say about many things

that have become clear and essential to us. Nonetheless, it does know the meaning of marriage for
the person, society, and Church. In the New Testament
something new comes into existence that has acted as
a force to shape subsequent history.

§ 4 The Greco-Roman Environment[48]

While marriage in the Greek world was contracted through a binding consent (of both families), a religious consecration could also mark the beginning of it. According to Plato (*Republic* 461A; see also *Laws* 841D), priestesses and priests and indeed the entire state should offer sacrifices and prayers at every wedding. For through the offspring it produces, marriage serves the family and the fatherland. Both Plato and Aristotle therefore recommend family planning and, in some circumstances, abortion and the exposure of newborn infants (§9).

In Rome, too, most marriages were contracted through agreements valid in civil law and could be dissolved in the same way. But marriages could also be solemnly contracted with religious rites in the presence of a priest. Bigamy in the strict sense was not permitted by Roman law. In imperial Rome, of course, morals and morality certainly became rather free and easy. Public opinion allowed a husband to have extramarital sexual relations, though not with a married woman, while extramarital relations on the part of a wife were regarded as adultery.

Above the reality of marriage stood the ideal. During the centuries before the coming of Christianity, the philosophers, especially the Stoics, endeavored to develop the moral dimension of the individual person and of society at large, and therefore of marriage as well. An early witness to this effort is the work *On Marriage* by Antipater of Tarsus (ca. 150 B.C.).[49] He says that in marriage "true and sincere benevolence," "the closest kind of communion," and "the highest degree of affection" are realized. While other types of communion do not transcend in fact the level of simple juxtaposition, marriage is "a complete commingling and interpenetration as of wine and water." "The married couple, and they alone, share not only their possessions, children (the dearest thing any human being has), and souls, but even their very bodies." "A person who in marriage acquires another self as it were—be it man or woman—will do everything much more easily and effortlessly."

In the first century A.D. there lived at Rome the Stoic C. Musonius Rufus, whose teaching was recorded by his students.[50] The only sexual intercourse he regarded as morally licit was in marriage, where its purpose was the procreation of children (no. 12). The model marriage is one "in which the relationship of mutual care is full and complete, and both spouses show this concern for one another; in fact, each strives to excel and outdo the other. Such a communion is truly beautiful" (no. 13A). The mightiest of the deities protect marriage, namely, Hera, the foundress of marriage, Eros, and Aphrodite. For this reason it behooves even philosophers to marry (no. 14). Musonius rejects the practices of limiting the number of children, abortion, and the exposure of infants (no. 15AB).

One of Musonius' students was Epictetus, whose lectures were likewise written down by a student. He outlaws unnatural lust as well as adultery (*Discourses* IV, 2, 9). Even lascivious desires are wrong: "No woman should seem more beautiful to you than your wife"

(*Discourses* III, 7, 21) Philosophy requires that we discipline even our thoughts: "You are a fragment of God himself! Do you forget this relationship? Will you not remember who you are, as you engage in sexual intercourse? You carry God within you and do not realize that you defile him by your impure thoughts no less than by your unclean actions" (*Discourses* II, 8, 11-12).

The Greek philosopher Plutarch (ca. 45-124 A.D.) devoted a number of books to the themes of marriage and women: an artistic dialogue *On Love (Erotikos)*, *Conjugal Precepts, On the Virtues of Women*.[51] By natural disposition and native endowment, man and woman are ordered to one another and are equal in regard to rights and duties. Women have in a special way "a natural capacity for loving attention to others; they are like fruitful earth in their receptivity to friendship" (769C). "In marriage, to love is a higher value even than to be loved" (769D). Marriage is the most profound form of union and the purest kind of happiness known to human beings. Children are the wealth and joy of the house. True eros ennobles the actions of Aphrodite (759F) and brings about the full union proper to marriage (769F). "For the sake of the communion that results in procreation Nature makes even the gods feel the need of love" (770A).

We must not overlook the great female figures of Greek poetry, such women as Andromache, Penelope, Iphigenia, Antigone, Alcestis, Medea, and Phaedra. The tragic poets portray love and marriage with consummate art and persuasive truthfulness. The engraver's stylus and the sculptor's chisel have likewise created unforgettable images of woman. The erotic romances of late antiquity describe the various courses love takes, while the Roman elegy gives powerful expression to the experience of love, although the love here is not marital love.

In late antiquity, ascetic trends also made their appearance. As in the Old Testament (§§1.4; 2.8) and to an even greater degree, certain Greco-Roman views saw sexuality as subject to demonic forces and as a source of uncleanness (taboo). Sexual intercourse must therefore be avoided prior to cultic activity or else be counteracted by ritual ablutions (Tibullus, *Elegies* II, 1, 11-14[52]; Ovid, *Fasti* IV, 657). The priests and priestesses of the mystery religions are bound to abstain from sex before cultic activity. Isis "communicates her teaching to those who achieve divine perfection through a life of continual temperance in which they avoid immoderate eating and the deeds of Aphrodite and hold the reins tight against excess and carnal pleasure" (Plutarch, *Isis and Osiris* 351F). The devotees of Isis practice sexual continence on her feasts (Tibullus, *Elegies* I, 2, 23-26; Propertius, *Elegies* II, 33, 1-6). Plotinus, the great philosopher of late antiquity, never married (Porphyry, *Life of Plotinus* 9, 12) and taught that "there are no marriages in heaven" (*Enneads* III, 5, 2[15]). The principle followed in his school was: "The actions of Aphrodite defile" (Porphyry, *On Continence* 4, 20).

The Greek spirit was able, however, to rise above this constricting outlook. According to Diogenes

Laertius (*Lives of the Philosophers* VIII, 30, 43), when Theano, the Pythagorean philosopher, was asked how many days it took for a woman to become pure after intercourse, she answered that a woman is pure "after intercourse with her husband, immediately; after intercourse with another man, never." In the fourth century A.D., Iamblichus painted an idealized picture of the life and teaching of Pythagoras. He reports the philosopher as saying to women: "When you come from intercourse with your spouse, you have a divine right to visit the shrines that same day. But you have no such right after forbidden sexual relations" (*Life of Pythagoras* 11, 55).

§ 5. The Synoptic Gospels[53]

1. Jesus' Statement on Divorce

Beginning with sayings of the Lord that are handed down in the synoptic Gospels, the New Testament addresses reservations and criticisms to marriage as organized and lived in Israel. At the same time, it exhorts Christians to a new beginning that is based on the words and work of Christ.

In four passages (Mt. 5:32 = Lk. 16:18, probably from Q, the sayings-source; Mk. 10:11-12 and Mt. 19:9, in the Markan tradition), the Gospels report a statement of the Lord in which he rejects all divorce.[54]

The evidence suggests that the statement was handed down as an isolated saying and that the original words are most probably to be seen in their simplest form in Lk. 16:18: "Every one who divorces his wife and marries another commits adultery, and he who marries a woman divorced from her husband commits adultery." The background of the statement is the Old Testamental and Jewish law according to which the husband, and he alone, could dissolve his marriage. According to Jesus, adultery begins with the dismissal of the wife and is completed when the man enters upon a new marriage. If a man marries a divorced woman, he violates the still existing original marriage of that woman.

In Mt. 5:32 and 19:9, the original saying has been expanded through the introduction of the unchastity-clause. Mk. 10:11-12 presupposes Greco-Roman law, in which either husband or wife could dissolve the marriage. Paul, too, was familiar with the Lord's saying and quotes it in 1 Cor. 7:10 in a form according to which husband and wife are equals. Elsewhere (Rom. 7:1-14) Paul supposes that the marital union of two lives can be dissolved only by death.

In Mt. 5:32 and Lk. 16:18, the statement of Jesus has for its context discourses made up of individual sayings. In Mk. 10:2-12 (= Mt. 19:3-9), the statement of Jesus comes as the conclusion of a polemical discussion with the Pharisees. The Pharisees appeal to the Old Testamental and Jewish law of divorce as stated in Dt. 24:1 (§2.2.2). Over against this Jesus sets Gen. 1:27 and 2:24 as the expression of God's original will. It is quite possible, of course, that Jesus may in fact have gotten into a discussion of Dt. 24:1; nonetheless, the story as a whole perhaps reflects a discussion in the community about the new order of marriage and how it was to be defended against the synagogue.

The indication of place in Mk. 10:1 ("And he . . . went to the region of Judea and beyond the Jordan") is geographically unclear and probably represents not historical fact but the work of an editor. This fact was recognized by the tradition, which sought to improve matters, beginning with Mt. 19:2 and including some manuscripts of Mk. 10:1. The evangelist's efforts to create a framework are also to be seen in the remark that the crowds gathered and Jesus taught them as was his custom (so too in Mk. 1:22; 2:3; 4:1; 6:7; 11:17).

The Pharisees, who are the typical adversaries of Jesus, come on the scene as the opponents in the debate. They seek to "test" Jesus; this too is the attitude usually ascribed to them and is not to be taken here as authentic historical fact. The point of the discussion in Mk. 10:2-9 is to abrogate the practice of divorce that was allowed by the law of Moses. In its plan and development, however, the discussion is not immediately clear. The Pharisees ask: "Is it lawful for a man to divorce his wife?" (10:2). It is hardly permissible to infer from this that the questioners, and with them a part of the Jewish people, had doubts of conscience about whether the law and the practice of divorce were ultimately lawful and right. For the Pharisees there could be no question but that it was legitimate to divorce a wife. In other words, the question was probably only a way of starting the discussion.

Mt. 19:3 introduces a striking change: "Is it lawful to divorce one's wife for any cause?" The reference is to the question debated between the schools of early Judaism (§2.2.2). Matthew probably introduces this emendation deliberately.

The indication of place, "in the house," is unrelated to the context given (cf. 10:1), but is in the Markan style (Mk. 2:1; 7:17, 24; 9:28, 33). The thinking reflected in Mk. 10:11 is, in all probability, thoroughly Old Testamental and Jewish, since here it is the husband who divorces his wife and marries another; the formulation, however, is probably of a later date, since the juridical principle that reflected such thinking is quoted. Mk. 10:12, on the other hand, presupposes a Hellenistic and Roman background, since only there could a wife obtain a divorce from her husband.

In the polemical discussion in Mk. 10:3-8, there are three citations from the Old Testament: Dt. 24:1 is put on the lips of the Pharisees, and Gen. 1:27 and 2:24 on the lips of Jesus. Although the Gospels make it certain that Jesus lived in an ambience of the Old Testament as God's word and that he was constantly citing it,[55] nonetheless in this particular case of an Old Testament citation occurring in a statement of Jesus, the exegete will ask whether it is really Jesus who speaks here or rather a community that is theologizing on the basis of Scripture. The question is all the more relevant since in Mk. 10:6-9 the two citations are closely connected with each other. Is there a systematic biblical theology already at work here? Since Gen. 1:27 and 2:24 had already been brought together as a unit in Mal. 2:14-15 and Tb. 8:6, it is probable that Mk. 10:6-9 is giving expression to a Jewish biblical theology that had been taken over by Christians.

In Mk. 10:8, Gen. 2:24 is cited according to the Greek translation of the Old Testament: "The two shall become one flesh." The Hebrew text says only: "They shall become one flesh." This means that in Mk. 10:8 the Greek community is speaking. These considerations strengthen the probability that in Mk. 10:1-12 the scene presented has been constructed by an editor.

Mk. 10:1-12, along with Mt. 5:31 (both texts with their parallels) and 1 Cor. 7:10, shows that the community of Jesus' disciples, in contrast to Israel and also to the surrounding Greco-Roman world, rejected divorce. The early Church was convinced that in this rejection it was obeying the command of Jesus, and therefore it appealed to his own words. There can be no disputing that this stand was historically correct. Something new had begun. The evangelist recognizes this and gives expression to it in the antitheses of the Sermon on the Mount: "It was also said, 'Whoever divorces his wife, let him give her a certificate of divorce.' But I say to you that everyone who divorces his wife . . . makes her an adulteress" (Mt. 5:31-32).

The words of Jesus, then, are correctly interpreted in Mk. 10:2-12. In their argument for the right and practice of divorce, the adversaries of Jesus (Mk. 10:2-4) are speaking always of what is allowed; beyond this there seems nothing more to be said. They are interested only in the formal law according to which marriages can be validly contracted and validly dissolved. What is valid and right in the eyes of the law and its representatives is valid and right also for conscience and in the sight of God. It is to this outlook that Jesus responds (10:5-9).

The law of divorce given in Dt. 24:1-4 is highly questionable. Jesus describes it as a commandment of Moses. Like the entire law in Deuteronomy, the law of divorce is there given as God's commandment, but Jesus says that in fact Moses was the source of the commandment and that this last is therefore a man-made law. God's will and ordination are not expressed in their ideal purity in the law of Moses, but only in an imperfect way. The bill of divorce is a concession to human wickedness. In fact, it is even an indictment of this wickedness, and a revealing judgment on the hardness of heart of those who live in accordance with such a law.

The original will of God is not expressed in this later law but in the initial state of affairs that God had established. On the morning of creation, God's word and will had not yet become hidden and distorted, but still possessed their full splendor and power. Jesus now restores and proclaims this by appealing to the story of creation: "From the beginning of creation, 'God made them male and female'" (Mk. 10:6, citing Gen. 1:27). Jesus here gives greater emphasis to the words of Genesis, which in their original form say that man and woman were both created directly in God's image and therefore possess the same dignity; the manner in which Jesus cites the text brings out the fact that man and woman are the two parts of the one human being.

Consequently, the union of the sexes in marriage is God's ordinance and abiding work. "'For this reason a man shall leave his father and mother and be joined to his wife, and the two shall become one [flesh]' " (Mk. 10:7-8, citing Gen. 2:24). The Hebrew text says: "They shall become one flesh." The Greek text inflects the statement to emphasize the unity of the two. The new unity that is achieved through marriage is given priority over the most primitive of all human relationships, that of parents and children. The new relation transcends the old. The statement of Jesus speaks of the bodily union of the spouses; in biblical language, however, "flesh" means the whole person (§1.1). In marriage husband and wife become one human being, a unity of persons; a person is not divisible.

The story of creation, moreover, is not simply a report of an action that God did only once. Rather, it is God who now, today, unites spouses in marriage; every human marriage comes to pass because of his will. Divorce is an offense against the present will of God. The principle, "What God has joined together, let not man put asunder," applies to every marriage.

Since marriage is based on divine law, it is a communion of love and fidelity that is independent of any and every human law. Moreover, the duties and rights of marriage belong to husband and wife in the same way. Distinctions such as were maintained in Old Testamental and Jewish law on the basis of Dt. 24:1-4 (§2.2.2) are really not possible. Jesus brings out the right of the wife against the exercise of force on the part of the husband and against "legalized despotism."

Like the Gospel, the Damascus Document concludes that marriage with another woman while the former wife is still alive is "whoredom" (4, 20-21).

Here too the polygamy allowed by the law is unconditionally rejected.

Matthew makes it clear what marriage meant and required in the community of disciples, when, before the prohibition of divorce, he places sayings concerned with adultery (Mt. 5:27-30). "You have heard that it was said, 'You shall not commit adultery.' But I say to you that every one who looks at a woman lustfully has already committed adultery with her in his heart" (5:27-28). This saying is the second in the series of six antitheses in the Sermon on the Mount; the third will be the saying on divorce (5:31-32). This latter is to be read in the light of the saying about the lustful glance as an act of adultery. Divorce follows upon adultery and is by no means simply an unproblematic possibility allowed by the law. The saying in Mt. 5:27-28 is a further protection of woman against unscrupulous men.

The Old Testament, too, knows that the lustful look can be as evil as adultery (Job 31:1; etc.; §2.5). Adultery takes place in the heart. There are sins that the law cannot lay hold of and indict. That which society respects as faultless and honorable may in fact be a lie and an illusion. This hidden sin is threatened with hell (Mt. 5:29-30).

To the saying about the lustful gaze, Mt. 5:29-30 adds sayings about the eye and hand as sources of temptation. They begin with: "If your right eye causes you to sin, pluck it out and throw it away; it is better that you lose one of your members than that your whole body be thrown into hell." These warnings repeat threats of punishment for cultic offenses in the Old Testament (Ex. 19:21; Lev. 14:14-17, 20 28)

In Mk. 9:42-48 and Mt. 19:6-9, these sayings turn into sayings about the scandal that becomes a cause of sin. The members named as leading to sin in these latter two passages are hand, foot, and eye. Mt. 5: 27-30 shortens the list and changes the order. The evangelist here names the eye first in order to link the entire series with the saying about the lustful gaze in 5:28. While Mark speaks only of eye and hand, Matthew speaks of right eye and right hand, probably because "right," as opposed to "left," signified luck and greater value. A human being must be able to renounce even what is most dear when decisive action is required. Mt. 5:27-30 makes divorce far more than a mere legal case; it makes it a matter of radical decision.

2. The Blessing of the Children

The high value of marriage is still the subject when in both Mark (10:13-16) and Matthew (19:13-15) the story of the blessing of the children follows upon the sayings about divorce.[56] Coming as it does at this point, the story is intended by the evangelists as a statement about children as the form wealth takes in marriage.

Children are brought to Jesus "that he might lay hands on them and pray" (Mt. 19:13). Presupposed here is a beautiful Jewish custom: on the Sabbath parents used to bless their children, while on feast days they had them blessed by scribes as well. Here, then, Jesus is being asked to bless the children because he is the great, pious teacher. The disciples, however, seek to keep the children away from him: children are not the ones who should be coming to him, but adults, who can and will decide to follow him. But the Lord says that it is precisely to the children that the kingdom of God belongs.

Children are not called because they are supposedly innocent and pure. In the judgment of the Bible, every human being has an inheritance of evil (Gen. 8:21; Ps. 51:7). The Gospel tells us why children are so highly esteemed: "Whoever . . . receives the kingdom of God like a child . . ." (Mk. 10:15). The child is ready to receive; he is able to let gifts be given to him. He has not yet come to believe that he must first accomplish something; he does not rely on his works. When he is placed among the stronger and the wealthier, he expects everything from them. The child is thus an example of the persevering expectation that characterizes faith. God's kingdom can only be received as a gift. The child in the family embodies an abiding faith in, and openness to, the kingdom and its gifts. And because the kingdom is always coming to where it is awaited, the child also signifies the continual coming of the kingdom in the family.[57]

3. The Unchastity-Clause in Matthew 5:32 and 19:9

Only Matthew adds to the prohibition of divorce the clause "except for unchastity (*porneia*)" (5:32; 19:9). The clause was probably added by later tradition (or by the evangelist?) and reflects current Jewish marriage law, which (according to Dt. 24:1 as interpreted by the rabbis) not only allowed but ordered the husband to divorce a guilty wife (§2.2.2). Exegetical and dogmatico-juridical interpreters have given a great deal of thought to the unchastity-clause in Matthew. Catholic essays in interpretation seem, however, to have been codetermined by an effort to explain the text in a way that will harmonize with current canon law, which officially allows no divorce in a valid marriage. Consequently, the clause has been interpreted as referring to the "separation from bed and board" that Church law allows in extreme cases. Such casuistry, however, is certainly not in the mind of the evangelist.

Mt. 5:32 may be translated: "Everyone who divorces his wife—even the case of unchastity is excluded as a reason. . . ." We would then have to imagine Jesus making a gesture that expressed his rejection of even this exception. But this explanation breaks down when we attend to the language used in the Greek text.

Another interpretation given is that *porneia*, "unchastity," here means "idolatry," in accordance with an idiom used in the Old Testament (Hos. 1-3; Is. 3:2, 9; Ex. 16:15; Ps. 73:27). The sense would be that when the partners have different religions or when one of them apostatizes from the (Christian) faith, divorce would be allowed. But elsewhere in Matthew (15:20; 21:31), *porneia* always means adultery.

A recent essay in interpretation claims that in Mt. 5:32 and 19:9 *porneia* means a marriage forbidden by Old Testament law (Lev. 18:6-26), especially because of close kinship. The word *porneia* does have this meaning in Acts 15:20, 29; 21:25; Heb. 12:16. If this interpretation is maintained for the texts in Matthew, it would follow that in them pagans are being required to observe the Jewish laws governing marriage. But the word *porneia* does not occur in Lev. 18, and *porneia* would consequently be given an unusual meaning in Mt. 5:32 and 19:9. In addition, such a marriage with close relatives would be forbidden according to Old Testament law, and the man would not be free to dismiss his wife but would be obliged to dismiss her and dissolve the marriage.

The clause "except for unchastity" must therefore be understood as referring to unchaste behavior and adultery. Despite their high esteem for marriage, an esteem that Matthew, like the New Testament generally, expresses clearly enough, the New Testament community in this clause takes into account the harsh necessities of life. Once a marriage has been destroyed by the human sin of adultery, it cannot be declared still existent by an external law and in the face of the facts, and forced on the partners. Once the spouses have separated, then, in keeping with Old Testamental and Jewish law, at least the guiltless partner is allowed to enter a new marriage. Of course, even if separation may in the end prove to be the better solution, the New Testament commandment of love and forgiveness requires that efforts at reconciliation and a new beginning be made first. Especially to be noted is that Mt. 5:32 and 19:9, though they speak only of the man's right, cannot be used to allow him the unilateral right to pass judgment on his wife.

Catholic marriage law has not accepted the principle that adultery is grounds for divorce. At least this is the decision reached by the Council of Trent after a long period of hesitation. The Greek Orthodox Church, however, as well as the Uniate Catholic and Protestant Churches, acknowledge adultery as grounds for divorce.[58] The principle remains intact that man may not dissolve a marriage in which God has united man and woman.

4. Sin and Forgiveness
(Jesus and Women Who Were Sinners)

Contrasting with the strict demands Jesus makes in regard to marriage are accounts showing him as the friend of sinners and especially as the Savior who liberates women from the burden of serious sins. One such story is that of the anointing of Jesus by a woman who was a public sinner (Lk. 7:36-50).[59] As exegetes generally acknowledge, the story grew in the telling. In the process it became linked to the story of the woman who anointed Jesus at Bethany shortly before his death (Mk. 14:3-9). Even the words that interpret the event may have gradually been expanded. But the point of the story remains unchanged: Jesus accepts the loving homage of the sinful woman and places her ahead of the righteous. "Her sins, which are many, are forgiven, for she loved much" (Lk. 7:47). For the sake of human beings, Jesus disregards the moral judgment and law of society.

Another story is that of Jesus and the adulteress (Jn. 7:53-8:11).[60] The adversaries of Jesus declare that she should be stoned in accordance with Old Testament law (Dt. 22:20-24). Jesus protects her, however: "Let him who is without sin among you be the first to throw a stone at her." The men steal away, "beginning with the eldest"; Jesus absolves the woman and sends her away: "Go, and do not sin again."

In the time of Jesus, there was probably a debate going on about the validity of the death penalty for adultery as prescribed in Lev. 20:10 and Dt. 22:20-24. Jesus freely decides against the Old Testament law and its representatives. This story was shocking not only to contemporary Jews but to early Christians as well. For this reason it was not accepted into the early Gospels; only in the Gospel of John did it find a place, and an uncertain one at that.

The contrast between Jesus' strict demands and his readiness to forgive is explained by the fact that the purpose of "God's visitation" (Lk. 7:16) was not to judge men according to a law but to rescue them. In the last analysis, uprightness is always a gift; it is not merited by human effort. "The tax collectors and the harlots go into the kingdom of God before you" (Mt. 21:31-32).

5. The Parable of the Wedding

If we reflect on all the sayings of Jesus about marriage, we will be reminded that just as the rabbis used a wedding feast as an image of messianic joy and the splendor of the end-time and therefore would interrupt their teaching to share in the jubilation of a wedding, so Jesus too liked the image of a wedding. When others reproach him because his disciples do not fast, he answers that the present time, while he is with them, is a wedding feast for them, and therefore they cannot fast. The bridegroom is Jesus, just as God had been the bridegroom for the prophets (Is. 62:5).

Jesus compares the reign of God to the celebration of a wedding banquet that a king gives for his son (Mt. 22:1-10). The son is the Messiah; he is Jesus himself. In the parable of the ten virgins (Mt. 25:1-13), the wedding is an image of the heavenly kingdom; the bridegroom who comes and summons the virgins to the wedding is Jesus as Messiah and Judge.

A wedding is an image of joy and festivity; Christ accepts it and elevates it to the rank of a messianic and eschatological sign.

6. Reservations

The Gospel, which has such sublime things to say about marriage, also has sayings that express reservations. In the Gospel of Matthew, the saying about the indissolubility of marriage is followed by another about celibacy. "There are eunuchs [celibates] who have been so from birth, and there are eunuchs [celibates] who have been made eunuchs by men, and there are eunuchs [celibates] who have made themselves eunuchs for the sake of the kingdom of heaven" (Mt. 19:10-12).[61]

Devout Jews taught that there was an obligation to marry (§2.7), but Jesus speaks of possibilities of celibacy that occur in fact. There is a celibacy that has a physiological cause—these are celibates who were born that way. There is a celibacy due to human force and violence—these are the celibates whom other men have made celibate. And there is a celibacy that is freely willed for the sake of the kingdom of heaven. The reign of God presses upon us and is near at every moment; in fact, in Christ it is already truly here, even though hidden (Lk. 11:20). If Christ himself is the reign of God already begun, then "for the sake of the kingdom of heaven" means "for the sake of Christ."

There are human beings who direct all their powers and their whole lives to the reign of God that presses upon them and to its presence in Christ, so that they will not and cannot devote their energies to anything else or allow anything else to captivate them. The same point is expressed in other sayings such as this one: "Every one who has left houses or brothers or sisters or father or mother or children or lands, for my name's sake, will receive a hundredfold, and inherit eternal life" (Mt. 19:29). The reservation is thus an eschatological and Christological reservation.

The saying of Jesus in Mt. 19:12 speaks of eunuchs, or castrated persons. The Old Testament and Judaism speak of eunuchs only with contempt. Such persons could not belong to the community of God (Dt. 23:2). Even a castrated animal could not be used in a sacrifice (Lev. 22:24-25). Contempt for eunuchs also finds expression in Gal. 5:12 and Phil. 3:2. Is. 56:3-5 says that eunuchs will be accepted into the community of salvation in the end-time, but this is said as something almost unbelievable to show the magnitude of the salvation that is to come.

Here again, Jesus takes the side of those who are among the despised. God can and will choose even these. Being an object of contempt can change into a being called. But only those to whom insight is given can understand this (Mt. 19:11). In a similar manner

Paul speaks of celibacy as a possible charismatic gift (1 Cor. 7:7). Both marriage (Mt. 19:4-6) and celibacy can be God-given states of life.

Jesus speaks of those whom force exercised by men has made celibates (Mt. 19:12). The saying in its original sense probably refers to those who through a physical attack made on them have been rendered incapable of marriage. We will be justified, however, in understanding it in our time in a transferred sense of those whom constraining social and economic conditions, a political catastrophe such as war, or any of life's vicissitudes have forced to remain unmarried.

According to the statisticians, a third of the women in many European countries must remain unmarried against their will. Women are often the defenseless victims of the unnatural conditions of life in our society. It may be initially true, then, as the saying of Jesus has it, that this celibacy was forced upon human beings by their fellows and was not therefore originally a calling for them. But a celibacy that was initially endured unwillingly can be accepted, perhaps first as a painful sacrifice, but then also as something positive, along with the possibilities and tasks that the celibate can fulfill.

The Gospel reports other sayings that express reservations about marriage. The Sadducees asked Jesus a bizarre question about the husband to whom a woman would belong at the resurrection if she had married seven brothers in succession. Jesus answered: "When they rise from the dead, they neither marry nor are given in marriage, but are like the angels in heaven" (Mt. 12:18-27, at v. 25). A new eon is coming in which there will be no more marrying. Marriage belongs to a world that is subject to death, and therefore it will have no place in the new transformed world of those who have risen from the dead. These last will be spiritual like the angels.

This saying of Jesus contradicts the usual Jewish image of the future, according to which it was expected that the new eon would bring the utmost heightening of joy in marriage and children. But ideas similar to those of Jesus are expressed in Jewish apocalyptic literature. For example, we read in the Syriac Apocalypse of Baruch (51, 10): "After resurrection and judgment the just will dwell on the heights of that world and be like the angels." A rabbi says of the just in heaven: "They do not eat or drink; they do not reproduce themselves but live forever."[62]

Jesus says that marriage will cease. Perhaps his words are a hint that the coming end is already affecting the present age and setting limits upon marriage as upon everything else. This does not mean that marriage does not now have its meaning and riches, but that it has them in the same manner as the flowers of which Jesus speaks, which are glorious today but tomorrow will wither away.

Another saying that offers food for reflection is to be found in the parable of the great banquet as reported in Luke (14:15-24). The banquet has been prepared, and the king sends his messengers to invite the guests, but they do not come. In the parable as told by Matthew (22:1-10), it is said only that "they made light of it and went off, one to his farm, another to his business" (22:5). In Luke, however, the excuses of each are given: "I have bought a field," "I have bought five yoke of oxen," "I have married a wife."

The banquet of the parable stands for the coming reign of God. The Gospel of Luke says that business, work, and the acquisition of possessions keep men from entering under the reign of God. This is a first point that would not be immediately intelligible to the hearers, inasmuch as Israel was persuaded that the pious man is blessed by God in his work and his striving after profit and wealth.

Even more striking is the idea that marriage can keep a man from entering under the reign of God. Is this idea not wholly alien to Israel's teaching and faith, according to which marriage was established by God himself? The statements in Luke seem so un-Jewish that we may ask whether we are not listening to a Christian expansion of something the Lord had said. A comparable idea is to be found in 1 Cor. 7:32-39, where Paul says that the unmarried man is solicitous for the affairs of the Lord, whereas the married man is solicitous for the affairs of the world and is therefore a divided man.

Another saying of Christ issues a warning by means of a reference to the generation that experienced the flood: "They ate, they drank, they married, they were given in marriage, until the day when Noah entered the ark, and the flood came and destroyed them all" (Lk. 17:26-27). The world stands before imminent judgment, but forgets this amid its secular activity. Part of this secular activity, however, is marrying and being given in marriage. The point is not that eating, drinking, and marrying are evil in them-

selves and forbidden, but rather that as man uses and
enjoys what the natural world provides, he can neglect
God's urgent call and thereby become liable to judgment.

To these texts of Luke's Gospel that speak of the
ambiguities of marriage, other comparable sayings
can be added. Mt. 10:37 speaks of the decision required
of a disciple: "He who loves father or mother more
than me is not worthy of me; and he who loves son
or daughter more than me is not worthy of me." And
Mt. 19:29: "And every one who has left houses or
brothers or sisters or father or mother or children or
lands, for my name's sake, will receive a hundredfold,
and inherit eternal life."

These sayings take a significantly different form
in Luke. Lk. 14:26: "If any one comes to me and does
not hate his own father and mother and wife and children and brothers and sisters . . . he cannot be my
disciple." Lk. 18:29: "Truly, I say to you, there is no
man who has left house or wife or brothers or sisters
or parents or children, for the sake of the kingdom
of God, who will not receive manifold more in this
time, and in the age to come eternal life." To both
sayings Luke has added renunciation of a wife, that
is, of marriage. His Gospel tends to lay special emphasis on the crisis that comes upon marriage in the presence of the kingdom of God that is pressing upon us.
Is it perhaps the individual evangelist who speaks
here, while the New Testament as a whole also contains other motifs and value-judgments?

The Gospel affirms and proclaims the world to be
God's created order, and marriage to be part of that

order. But there is another order that surpasses the order of creation and can abrogate it, namely, the order we enter into for the sake of the oncoming reign of God.

7. Divorce According to Church Law

The saying of Jesus that a marriage brought about by God cannot be dissolved by men has become a canon in the Church's legal code: "A marriage which is valid, sacramental, and consummated cannot be dissolved by any human power or by any cause whatsoever, save by death" (canon 1118). The indissolubility of marriage is here regarded as a principle of divine law.

This legal statement raises some important questions, however.[63] The Lord's saying about the indissolubility of marriage occurs in Mt. 5:31 as one in a series of antitheses that are part of the Sermon on the Mount and embody the highest moral demands and duties. Can these demands and duties be formulated in juridical terms as paragraphs of a legal code? Another of the antitheses says that anyone who is angry with his brother or curses him is liable to judgment (Mt. 5:22-23). No one has ever thought of turning this into a set of legal principles. Still another antithesis forbids taking oaths: "But I say to you, Do not swear at all" (5:33-34). Nonetheless, in Christian society and in the Church, oaths are constantly being required and given. In his confrontation with Jewish law, did Jesus not remove marriage from the sphere of human disputes and ground it in the simple original order established by God?

In its regulation of marriage, the Church claims the right to determine certain cases in which divorce is possible. In so doing, it interprets and, it would seem, also modifies the principle that a marriage validly contracted in accordance with natural law or, for Catholic Christians, in accordance with Church law, is indissoluble by divine law.

The Church has issued a number of prescriptions, some of them changeable, regarding the form to be followed in the contracting of a marriage. If these prescriptions are not observed, a marriage can be null and void from the outset.

Church law also distinguishes between valid sacramental marriages and valid sacramental marriages that have been consummated as well. Only the latter are regarded as indissoluble. The pope can dissolve a marriage that is valid and sacramental but not consummated. Such a marriage is dissolved by law when a solemn religious profession supervenes.[64]

Adopting Old Testament tradition, Church law establishes impediments to marriage.[65] A beginning of this practice may be found in 1 Cor. 5:1-5, where Paul sharply criticizes relations between stepmother and stepson. Some of the impediments to marriage are based on natural law, others are historically conditioned. When they are the kind of impediments that separate or divide (diriment impediments), they make a marriage contract invalid and void from the outset, even if the couple are not aware of them.

Church law acknowledges a permanent or temporary separation from bed and board when a marriage has become admittedly intolerable. As a result of such a separation, marriage ceases to be a community of life, and only the formal marriage bond is left, but this prevents the contracting of any new marriage (Code of Canon Law, canons 1128-31).

On the basis of the "Pauline privilege" and "in favor of the faith," a Catholic court can dissolve a naturally valid marriage between non-baptized persons if one spouse receives baptism and then asks for the dissolution of the marriage (canons 1120-27). This law is derived from 1 Cor. 7:12-15, where Paul allows a Christian spouse to abandon his or her marriage when the unbeliever wants the dissolution, and a peaceful life together is no longer possible. However, Paul advises the Christian spouse not to dissolve the mixed marriage, but to remain in it, if possible.

The "Petrine privilege" was elaborated as a prolongation of the Pauline privilege.[66] It says that the pope, as successor of St. Peter, has the power to dissolve, in an act of clemency, a marriage valid according to the natural law or a Christian marriage[67] or even a Catholic marriage. In recent years the use of this privilege has greatly increased. A canonical examination and testing of the principles invoked and their application would hardly be feasible now.

In every diocese of the Catholic Church and within the Roman Curia, there are various marriage tribunals that attend to the regulating of marriage. In accordance with the principle that a valid marriage is indissoluble, divorces are not granted in such cases, but it may be determined in certain circumstances that a marriage was invalid from the outset, and the partners are therefore freed through an annulment.

This is happening with increasing frequency, at the request of one or both spouses. The reason often given for the annulment is a lack of form in contracting the marriage (that is, neglect of various prescriptions regarding form or of diriment impediments). Another reason may be the lack of a true marital intention from the outset.

§ 6. The Letters of Paul[68]

1. 1 Corinthians 6:16-17 (Adam and Eve)

It was through the theology of early Judaism (§1.5) that Paul received the story of the creation and fall according to Gen. 1-3. He interpreted the biblical text with the help of the rabbinic methods and views he had learned during his own education for the rabbinate. Since we have but an inadequate knowledge of these presuppositions, it is to some extent difficult for us to understand the Apostle's exegesis of the texts.

Like the Gospels (§5.1), Paul sees in the passage on the divine institution of marriage (Gen. 2:24) an expression of the unity of the spouses. In 1 Cor. 6:16-17 he uses Gen. 2:24 to warn against sexual union with a prostitute: "Do you not know that he who joins himself to a prostitute becomes one body with her? For, as it is written, 'The two shall become one [flesh].' But he who is united to the Lord becomes one spirit with him." Moreover, God will raise up the body (1 Cor.

6:4), and the body of the Christian is, in addition, a member (of the body) of Christ (1 Cor. 6:15) and a temple of the Holy Spirit (1 Cor. 6:19). The Christian must therefore not allow his and Christ's body to be one flesh with a prostitute. Rather, the Christian must cleave to the Lord, in order to be one spirit with him (1 Cor. 6:17).

The biblical and Pauline opposition of flesh and spirit plays a role in these statements. In Paul's emphatic use of the phrase, "one flesh" means not only bodily union but a spiritual and personal union as well. This conclusion emerges from the contrasting statement, namely, that the Christian is one spirit with the Lord.

2. 1 Corinthians 11:2-16
(Man and Woman as Image of God)

Paul repeatedly treats of the person and history of Adam. Through the disobedience of one man, Adam, sin and death entered the world. In addition, Adam's descendants made this sad fate their own by their personal guilt. Yet the grace of one man, Jesus Christ, won justification and life in far greater measure for all (Rom. 5:12-21; 1 Cor. 15:22).

Paul says nothing in this context about Eve's share of the guilt, but he does speak emphatically of her sin and fall when in 1 Cor. 11:2-16 he gives an extended explanation of the biblical account of creation. His intention in this passage is to describe the conduct and role of women in the liturgy. To this end, the question of women covering their heads becomes very important in his eyes.

In discussing what may seem to us a rather unimportant question, Paul brings in considerations from the theology of creation (11:8-9), from tradition (11:2), and from natural law (11:14). His rule that women should wear a veil during divine services is still followed today in some Roman Catholic countries. Canon 1262 of the Code of Canon Law would have women be present in church only if they are modestly dressed and their heads are covered.

When Paul requires women to veil their heads during the liturgy, his intention is to make obligatory the Jewish custom that women should be veiled when they appear in public. In the Greek world, on the other hand, freedom was the rule in this matter. The Apostle, however, concludes that an unveiled woman is like a prostitute who has her hair shorn as a sign of her trade (11:6).

A woman must cover her head as a sign of subordination to her husband. "The head of the woman is her husband," says Paul (11:2), probably with Gen. 3:16 in mind: "He [your husband] shall rule over you." The statement that "he [man] is the image and glory of God," while woman is the glory of man (11:7), is probably a paraphrase of Gen. 1:27, where it is said that God created man after his image as male and female. In keeping with Gen. 2:18, 22-23, Paul also says that "man was not made from woman, but woman from man" and that "neither was man created for woman, but woman for man." As the being whom God created first (Gen. 2:7), the man is directly the image and glorious reflection of God's majesty, while the woman is the glory only of the man because she was created from him (Gen. 2:22).

Paul supplements the biblical statements with ideas based on the Jewish understanding of them. If the man is the head of the woman, Christ is the head of every man, and God is the head of Christ (11:3). "A man ought not to cover his head, since he is the image and glory of God" (11:7). Does "head" here mean man's own bodily head, or does it mean God as his invisible head? In any case, the woman must veil her head because she is the glory only of the man.

Greek philosophy, especially such as was dependent on Plato, taught that things are hierarchically ordered images of the divine ideas. Judeo-Hellenistic sapiential teaching accepted this notion and therefore described man as image of God (Wis. 2:23; Sir. 17:1). Wisdom itself is "a pure emanation of the glory of the Almighty. . . . a reflection of eternal light . . . an image of his goodness" (Wis. 7:25-26). Philo developed this speculation still further.

Paul makes use of the concepts of glory and reflected splendor (11:7) and adds another from contemporary (gnostic?) language when he speaks of the universal head (11:3). Using these concepts, he develops his teaching on Christ. Christ is the image of God (2 Cor. 4:4). God is the head of Christ because Christ is God's eternal Son (Rom. 1:3-4). To say that Christ is the head of the man probably means that the man stands in a relationship of immediacy and openness to Christ, who summons him to believe and serve, whereas the woman depends on man as mediator.

1 Cor. 11:10 makes a very unusual statement, the

explanation of which is not certain: "A woman ought
to have an authority [LXX; "veil," RSV] on her head,
because of the angels." According to this, the veil is
a sign of the authority on the head of the woman,
insofar as this veil signifies her subordination to her
husband or to God.[69]

The reason, however, why the woman must wear
this authority on her head is "the angels." Is Paul referring to the holy angels who are regarded as present
in the community and who are offended by every
impropriety? Such an interpretation would remind
us of the Qumran Rule of the Congregation, which
prescribes that the sick and the crippled are not to
take part in the liturgical assembly because "holy
angels are in their community" (1 QSa 2:3-11). Or
are the "angels" in this case the demonic powers that
lust after women, seduce them, and imperil them, so
that women must be protected against them by a veil?

Paul then brings in an argument from natural law.
"Does not nature itself teach you that for a man to
wear long hair is degrading to him, but if a woman
has long hair, it is her pride?" (11:14-15). In antiquity,
it was chiefly the Stoic philosophers who used the
concept of natural law in ethics. They claimed that
anyone who lived according to nature was living in
accordance with God's law. Paul's arguments here
will hardly seem conclusive to us, since the way in
which women wear their hair is simply a matter of
fashion.

The Apostle himself is probably aware in the end
that all his proofs are inadequate in this question of
the veil. Therefore he finally appeals to the custom

now followed in the Church: "If any one is disposed to be contentious, we recognize no other practice, nor do the churches of God" (11:16).

What Paul says in 1 Cor. 11 about the relationship of man and woman will strike us as culturally conditioned to a great extent. He seems to overlook the emphasis on the equality of man and woman in the story of creation (Gen. 1:27, 33). Indeed, his own stress on the subordination of woman is contradicted by two considerations he himself offers. One is from the Gospel and Christology: "Nevertheless, in the Lord woman is not independent of man nor man of woman" (1 Cor. 11:11). This is an application of. what is put in radical form in Gal. 3:28: "There is neither Jew nor Greek, there is neither slave nor free, there is neither male nor female; for you are all one in Christ Jesus."

The other consideration is from natural law and the theology of creation: "As woman was made from man, so man is now born of woman. And all things are from God" (1 Cor. 11:12). 1 Cor. 11:8b (the woman comes from the man) and 11:12b (the man is born of the woman, but everything is from God) really contradict each other. The most important thing, however, is that in this very same context Paul grants the Christian woman in the community the right to preach and to speak a liturgical prayer (1 Cor. 11:5; §12.5). Here he transcends his Jewish limitations.

Paul speaks on one occasion of Eve's being led astray. His concern at this point is to protect the virginal purity of the community, that is, its adherence to Christ. "I am afraid that as the serpent deceived Eve by his cunning, your thoughts will be led astray from a sincere and pure devotion to Christ" (2 Cor. 11:3). Since he speaks so emphatically of the damage done to virginal purity, the exegete asks whether he is here following Jewish tradition which reads into Gen. 3 the idea that the serpent seduced Eve into unchastity. This tradition is attested in the apocalyptic literature (Apocalypse of Abraham 237; Slavonic Enoch 31, 6) and in Jewish teaching. If Paul is indeed following this tradition, he is not really applying the myth to the Church, as though the Church had been led into immorality, but is rather warning her against falling away from Christ in any way.

3. 1 Corinthians 7 (Marriage and Celibacy)

Like the Gospels, the writings of the apostles must inevitably deal with the subject of marriage and its proper order.

Paul discusses the matter at length in 1 Cor. 7. We will recall from this chapter such sentences as these: "It is well for a man not to touch a woman" (7:1). "Because of the temptation to immorality, each man should have his own wife and each woman her own husband" (7:2). "It is better to marry than to be aflame with passion" (7:9). "In view of the impending [or: present] distress it is well for a person to remain as he is [i.e., unmarried]" (7:26). "If you marry, you do not sin" (7:28). "The unmarried man [and the unmarried woman] is anxious about the affairs of the Lord, how to please the Lord, but the married man [or woman] is anxious about worldly affairs, how to please his wife [or her husband]" (7:32–34). "The unmarried woman or girl is anxious about the affairs of the Lord,

how to be holy in body and spirit" (7:34). If engaged
persons are unsure whether they should marry or
whether it might not be better for them to remain
single, Paul advises them to marry "if it has to be." "It
is no sin." "But whoever is firmly established in his
heart, being under no necessity but having his desire
under control . . . will do well" not to marry. "He who
marries his betrothed does well; and he who refrains
from marriage will do better" (7:36-38).

Does Paul not fail to do justice to marriage in these
passages? It is not only his critics who ask this question.
His friends, too, have asked it and are asking it still.

As a matter of fact, it takes an effort to understand
the text. We must bear in mind its occasion, its intention, and its purpose. Paul is answering questions put
to him by his Corinthian community in a letter that
their messengers had brought to him during a lengthy
stay of his at Ephesus (1 Cor. 16:17). In his answer he
repeatedly refers to this letter (1 Cor. 7:1, 30; 8:1; 12:1;
16:1). His intention is not to provide a complete Christian doctrine of marriage. What he says is conditioned
by the questions he is answering and by the theological
and ecclesial situation in Corinth.

In its letter the Corinthian community asked,
among other things, what Christians must hold regarding marriage and sexuality. It seems that there
existed in the community (probably along with a
prudent middle-of-the-road position) some extremist
views. Many were of the opinion that the Christian
had a right to sexual license, because in comparison
with the Spirit bestowed in baptism, the body was
insignificant, and immorality had no effect on the

spirit (1 Cor. 6:12-20). Others, however, maintained that the Christian ideal was abstention from marriage and from the exercise of the sexual function. Paul responds to this second opinion in 1 Cor. 7.

In late antiquity, very diverse judgments were passed on marriage (§4; §9). Many spoke of it with supreme contempt, while other views downgraded marriage and called for abstention from it or at least continence within it. In the Greek world, philosophical considerations also played a part. According to the philosophy of Plato, the body was evil, the spirit good. Aristotle and the Stoics disparaged sexuality because its passions disturbed the calm of the wise man. At most, marriage was to be entered into as a duty to the nation. Summarizing such views, Stobaeus declared in the fifth century A.D.: "It is good not to marry" (*Eclogae* 4, 22, 28). Weariness with marriage and pessimism about it were fashionable. The divorce rate had risen to a dangerous level.

It may be that the questioning and uncertainty of the Corinthians were influenced by such attitudes and by gnostic ideas as well. In keeping with its dualistic worldview, gnosticism disowned the world and advised men, for the sake of true knowledge (gnosis), to practice asceticism in regard to food and the use of sex. For example, the Corpus Hermeticum (probably first century A.D.) says: "With the knowledge of God came the knowledge of joy. Next to joy I put continence. O delightful power! Let us accept it with glad good will!" (13, 8-9). Moreover, there were tendencies to sexual asceticism in the Judaism of Paul's day (§1.4; §2.8). In addition, there may have been motives supplied by a genuine, even if immoderate, Christian religious feeling. Thus there were probably Christians who regarded marriage and the use of sex as a stain on their holiness and a drag on their spiritual striving, and therefore were afraid of them. We can infer this from Paul's response in 1 Cor. 7:5, 14. It is along these general lines that we may explain the movements at Corinth that were hostile to marriage. In opposition to them, Paul had to defend the right to marry and the institution of marriage.

In 1 Cor. 7:1 Paul refers to the letter the Corinthians had written to him: "Now concerning the matters about which you wrote: It is well for a man not to touch a woman." Some exegetes suppose, as Origen and Tertullian may have done earlier, that Paul is here quoting the Corinthians' letter. In other words, it is the Corinthians who asserted that it is good for man not to touch a woman.[70] And yet this expedient hardly enables us to dissociate Paul from this harsh statement. "It is good" is a typically Pauline phrase (1 Cor. 7:8, 26; Rom. 14:20-21; Gal. 3:18). And in words that are certainly his own, Paul describes sexual asceticism as good and as the better thing (1 Cor. 7:8, 26, 38).

When Paul answers the questions of the Corinthians, he presupposes, as a Jew and especially as a theologically trained former Pharisee (Phil. 3:5), that the law contained in the Bible represents God's commandment. Gen. 1 and 2, in which it is reported that God instituted and blessed marriage in paradise, have abiding validity in his eyes. The Apostle frequently cites decisive sentences from Gen. 1 (Gal. 3:28) and Gen. 2 (1 Cor. 6:16; 11:7-9; 15:45, 47) as proof; thus we can see how the account of creation is always present in his mind. Thus, according to Rom. 7:1-3, marriage is a divine institution and law.

Paul is realistic about creation and man when he says that because of the danger of immorality each man should have his own wife and each woman her own husband (1 Cor. 7:2, 5). His words are sober, almost offensively so. The rabbis, too, taught that marriage is a protection against lust and immorality.[71] But then, do not the psychologists and sociologists say the same thing when they are forced to recognize that in marriage the human sexual drive reaches its goal and its repose, so that society is protected against disorders? We may recall Martin Luther's words: marriage is "a hospital for the diseased."[72]

The meaning of 1 Cor. 7:6 is not unequivocally clear. In fact, three interpretations are proposed. Some exegetes connect the verse with only one or the other part of verse 5. Then Paul would either be expressing a concession, not a command, that continence be observed for a time, or expressing a concession, not a command, that marital relations be resumed after the period of continence. But according to the third interpretation, 7:6 should rather be connected with the whole section 7:1-5, so that Paul is saying that marriage itself is conceded, not commanded. Paul is not commanding marriage, as the rabbis do who declare it a duty (§2.7); he is simply allowing it. There is nothing else he can say, since there must also exist in the community the possibility and right of celibacy.

The spouses, Paul is saying, each have the right to, and can ask for, the other's "conjugal obligations"

(7:3, NAB). This is the language and conviction of his time. According to Ex. 21:10, the husband owes his wife "her food, her clothing [and] her marital rights."[73] The "obligations" in 1 Cor. 7:3 are grounded in the created order and the natural law. This is also the sense of the verb "ought" in 1 Cor. 11:7 and 2 Cor. 12:14. But the same verb is also used for a duty based on love (Rom. 13:8; 15:1, 27). In fact, precisely with regard to marriage it is said in Eph. 5:28 that "even so husbands should love their wives." Is this meaning now also present in the term "obligations" in 1 Cor. 7:3?

Paul also argues that neither husband nor wife can freely dispose of his/her own body (1 Cor. 7:4). The least he is saying is that the marital rights and obligations of husband and wife are the same, and that therefore it is not simply a question of the wife serving the husband's desire. In addition, should we not also consider the fact that "body" (*soma*), when it conveys the sense of the Hebrew *basar*, means not only the physical body but the entire person (in accordance with Mk. 10:8, when Gen. 1:24 is cited; §1.1)? At a deeper level, then, is Paul not saying that the spouses are bound wholly to one another? Then 1 Cor. 7:5 acquires its full meaning: "Do not refuse one another"; at most, "by agreement for a season, that you may devote yourselves to prayer" may the spouses desist from intercourse.

The rabbis can praise the Jew for renouncing marital relations for a time for·the sake of studying the law, but according to them, the decision in this matter belongs to the husband and only to him.[74] Paul, on the other hand, presupposes that husband and wife are in agreement on the matter. The Testament of Naphtali is inspired by the same idea when it says: "There is a time for marital intercourse and a time to be continent in order to pray" (8, 8). According to Paul, such abstinence is not to be maintained over a long period, so that the marriage would really be abrogated on ascetical grounds. When he refuses such long-term abstinence "because of your lack of self-control" (1 Cor. 7:5), this is hardly to be taken as meaning that Paul would see in marriage evidence of the spouses' lack of self-control. Rather, the Apostle is warning spouses about the unbridled desires that may be aroused when asceticism is practiced.

To the unmarried and the widowed, Paul says that "it is better to marry than to be aflame with passion" (1 Cor. 7:8-9). He also warns against experiments and any use of force, for these can only end in disaster. The Church must be ready, in the advice she gives as well as in her law, to listen with all humility to these earnest words of Paul.

A text such as 1 Cor. 7:4 may be the ultimate basis for the definition given in the Code of Canon Law (canon 1081.2): "The marital consent is an act of the will whereby each partner gives the right to his or her own body and accepts the right to the body of the other. The right is perpetual and exclusive and relates to acts that are of themselves suitable for the begetting of children." This legal language shows a lack of sensitivity. It says that the essence of marriage is a reciprocal legal claim, and specifically a legal claim to another's body. But in fact the essence of marriage is rather the will to give and dedicate oneself in self-forgetfulness.

The object of this self-dedication is not just the body but the whole of a person's life and being.

The Second Vatican Council used quite different language in its Pastoral Constitution on the Church in the Modern World. Article 48 describes marriage as an "intimate partnership of life and . . . love." Article 49 says that "married love . . . is an affection between two persons rooted in the will and it embraces the good of the whole person; it can enrich the sentiments of the spirit and their physical expression with a unique dignity."[75] In his commentary on these articles, Bernard Häring observes: "We can only hope that such humiliating language [as is found in CIC 1081.2] will also disappear from canon law. 'Right to the body' comes down from a time when the wife was still listed with the husband's possessions. Merely to emphasize its mutual character scarcely improves matters."[76]

Old Testament law, contemporary discussion among Jews, and daily life all made Paul familiar with the law of divorce and questions concerning it. He was also familiar, however, with the Lord's words rejecting divorce (words also found several times in the synoptic tradition; see Mk. 10:5-8 and parallels; §5.1). For Paul and the community, this saying of the Lord has already decided the question of divorce: "To the married I give charge, not I but the Lord, that the wife should not separate from her husband . . . and that the husband should not divorce his wife" (1 Cor. 7:10-11). Thus the law of divorce as maintained in Judaism and in the ancient world generally is rejected in principle.

On the other hand, the saying of Jesus is not to be

taken as an inflexible legal principle; it must be applied
to real life. Paul first considers the cases in which Christian spouses in the community have separated, either
(we must supply here what is left unsaid) before they
entered the community or after they received baptism.
Paul now modifies the prohibition of divorce contained in the saying of the Lord. The separated wife
(only she is mentioned, but this is probably by way
of example) can remain separated from her husband
or she may be reconciled to him; in either case she has
no right to marry again (1 Cor. 7:11).

Frequently, perhaps even normally, marriages in
the communities were in the beginning marriages
between a Christian and a Jewish or pagan spouse—
in other words, mixed marriages involving two religions. Could a Christian continue to live in such an
intimate community of life with an unbeliever? After
all, Christianity was being forced to struggle with
all its might against the predominantly pagan world
around it and to separate itself from that world.

Israel, too, had been forced to raise this question
repeatedly in the course of its history. The law forbade
mixed marriages (Ex. 34:15-16). The struggle against
the paganism of Moab (Num. 25:1-10) and Canaan
(Jg. 3:5-6; Dt. 7:1-14; 1 Kg. 11:11-12; 16:31) made
it necessary to prohibit mixed marriages with these
peoples. After the return from the Babylonian Exile,
it was discovered that mixed marriages had become
common among the diverse peoples who had meanwhile settled in the country. Ezra (9; 10) and Nehemiah
(10:31; 13:23-30), priests both, called for the dissolution
of these marriages. Even as late as the New Testament

period, the law as interpreted by the rabbis prohibited mixed marriages.[77] Philo, in his *On the Special Laws* (3, 29), issues an urgent warning against mixed marriages because of the danger that parents and children alike may apostatize.

Paul takes a position against this Jewish law and advises couples to remain in mixed marriages. The Corinthian churches were perhaps afraid that the pagan spouse might infect the Christian by means of the cult of demons. Paul assures them: "The unbelieving husband is consecrated through his wife, and the unbelieving wife is consecrated through her husband. Otherwise, your children would be unclean, but as it is they are holy" (1 Cor. 7:14). The word "holy" here, as used in both the Old and the New Testaments, does not have the moral meaning to which we are accustomed, that is, leading a sinless and, in that sense, holy life. "Holiness" originally meant consecration by God and acceptance into community with him, who is the radically Holy One (Is. 6:3).

Marital communion, then, is so powerful that the one spouse is consecrated by the other, and the children of the marriage are likewise consecrated. The sanctifying power of Christ is greater than the power of the world and its demons to render unholy. This fact is the basis of Christian freedom (1 Cor. 8:4-6).

For the sake of this freedom, Paul is desirous that every use of coercion be avoided. If it is not possible for a couple to live together in peace, the Christian spouse is no longer bound to common life (1 Cor. 7: 12-16), and the marriage may be broken up. Marriage is possible only when the communion it involves is freely accepted; marriage cannot be forced on people. Peace and freedom are God's will for everything (1 Cor. 7:15). More than an inflexible law is involved here, and God's primary will for us undercuts all deadly legalism. Paul does not say whether remarriage is to be allowed in such cases, but surely freedom entails it.

According to Paul, marriage is part of the order of creation and redemption, and is therefore from God. At the same time, he acknowledges and speaks of celibacy as another possible style of life. "I wish that all were as I myself am. But each has his own special gift from God, one of one kind and another of another" (1 Cor. 7:7). Paul lives a celibate life and calls celibacy a distinctive gift of grace. Celibacy is possible insofar as it is a calling, and only to that extent.

Moreover, although Paul has high regard for this calling, he also integrates it into the order proper to the Church. Celibacy may not vaunt itself as something supposedly extraordinary. For there are many other gifts of grace, as the Apostle shows in the lists he gives in Rom. 12:6-21 and 1 Cor. 12-14. Among these he names service, teaching, wisdom, knowledge, faith, power to heal and other powers, prophecy, interpretation, and, above all, love (1 Cor. 13) and the word that helps others (1 Cor. 14).

In Rom. 12:6-8 and 1 Cor. 12:4-11, 28-31, Paul lists a large number of charisms and yet does not include celibacy. The reason probably is that the charisms in these lists are conceived of as services to the community and thought of in relation to the community.

The charism of celibacy is of a different kind: a gift for the personal profit of the charismatic. This fact may also be taken as indicating the limited value of the charism.

In a situation of eschatological tension and excitement, marriage can become meaningless and impossible. That is what we are told in early Jewish apocalyptic literature (§2.8), and the New Testament says the same. There are those who remain celibate for the sake of the imminent kingdom of God (Mt. 19:12). Regarding the distress of the last days, Mt. 24:19 says: "Alas for those who are with child and for those who give suck in those days!" Paul, too, goes into some detail in basing celibacy on the expectation of the imminent end: "I think that in view of the impending distress it is well for a person to remain as he is. Are you bound to a wife? Do not seek to be free. Are you free from a wife? Do not seek marriage. But if you marry, you do not sin" (1 Cor. 7:26-27). The words "impending distress" in verse 26 can also be translated as "present distress" (cf. 1 Cor. 3:22; Rom. 8:28; Gal. 1:4), according as the eschatological time that brings the distress is declared to be near at hand or already here.

Paul repeats: "The appointed time [of the world] has grown very short; from now on, let those who have wives live as though they had none, and those who mourn as though they were not mourning, and those who rejoice as though they were not rejoicing, and those who buy as though they had no goods, and those who deal with the world as though they had no dealings with it. For the form of this world is passing away. I want you to be free from anxieties" (1 Cor. 7:29-32). Paul hoped that the return of Christ and the end of the ages were at hand, even if he did not teach this as an absolute fact. Therefore he says that the impending end has now relativized all values and thrown them into a crisis. He lists marriage and possessions, but also spiritual things such as sorrow and joy. His view is that in the short time still left, it is better not to marry. For anyone who is married will experience "affliction according to the outward man" in this time of eschatological distress.

Paul may have been deceived as far as the calendar reckoning of the end of the world was concerned, but it does not follow that what he says in 1 Cor. 7 loses its validity. It is uncertain and of no essential importance just when the day will come according to the calendar. The essential point is that faith looks to the day of the Lord which is pressing upon us and that the coming of God and Christ in judgment and grace is constantly occurring in time and within the world. The Church lives continuously in the hope, the expectation, and even the presence of her Lord's coming. Celibacy is the state in the Church that seeks to be free of all ties so that it may express constant readiness. Celibacy is the eschatological sign in the Church.

Paul expresses the same idea when he describes the Church as a virgin bride who goes to meet the Lord Jesus Christ: "I feel a divine jealousy for you, for I betrothed you to Christ to present you as a pure bride to her one husband" (2 Cor. 11:2). In relation to the church of Corinth, the Apostle is like the father of the bride who keeps jealous watch over her so that he may keep her untouched for the bridegroom until the wedding. The day of the Church's wedding and union with her Lord is the day of Christ's return at the end of time. In its visions the Apocalypse already sees the marriage that will take place at the fulfillment of the ages between the Lamb and the Church that is adorned like a glorious bride (14:4; 19:2, 7; 21:2, 9). In New Testament statements such as these, celibacy becomes Christian virginity that is gladly accepted and lived in faith.

In his expectation of the imminent end, Paul reflects on a number of situations. Should engaged people go ahead and marry? He says they should if their passions are strong. "They do not sin" if they marry. And yet, "he who marries his betrothed does well; [but] he who refrains from marriage will do better" (1 Cor. 7:36-38).[78] Paul here rejects the Jewish view that a betrothal is a legally binding act and obliges the fiances to marry, and that a betrothal is already as binding as a marriage.

So, too, a widow is free to marry, "but in my judgment she is happier if she remains as she is," Paul writes. If she does marry, let it be "in the Lord" (1 Cor. 7:39-40). Whatever Paul has precisely in mind here (he hardly means that a widow must marry a Christian and no one else), his words will lead to the principle that Christians should enter into marriage in the presence of the Church, that is, the act of marrying must follow Church order and law.

Paul goes on to consider celibacy as the possibility of belonging wholly to the Lord. The unmarried person concentrates on the affairs of the Lord and how to please him. The married person is preoccupied with the affairs of the world; the husband is concerned with pleasing his wife, and the wife her husband (1 Cor. 7:32-34). Would Christian spouses be inclined to ask Paul a few questions at this point? They would admit that every marriage brings problems that can absorb the spouses' attention and be a burden to them. But at the same time, do not the marital union and mutual love, the concern and fidelity of the spouses fulfill God's commandments, and especially the primary commandment of love? Cannot spouses, singly and together, be preoccupied with the affairs of the Lord? After all, as Paul himself indicates elsewhere, the members of the body of Christ are to be concerned for one another (1 Cor. 11:25).

As early as around 200 A.D., Clement of Alexandria, one of the first interpreters of this passage of Paul, asks: "Is it not possible, in harmony with God, to live so as to please a wife and at the same time to thank God? Is a married man not allowed, together with his wife, to be intent on the affairs of the Lord?" (*Stromata* III, 88, 2). On the other hand, does celibacy, as such and always, represent undistracted attention to, and freedom for, the Lord?

Paul does not take up any of these points here. Is he perhaps speaking as the apostle and prophet who must travel the countries of the world without resting in order to preach the gospel and establish churches during this final brief span of time, and therefore as one whom the ties of marriage could only hinder?

According to what Paul says in 1 Cor. 7:14, Christian marriage sanctifies. In 1 Cor. 7:34, on the other hand, he says of the virgin that she "is anxious about the affairs of the Lord, how to be holy in body and spirit," whereas the married woman is anxious about worldly affairs. In this second passage, however, it is not marriage that makes unholy (this would contradict 1 Cor. 7:14), but the affairs of the world and anxiety about them, since they draw men away from God, the radically Holy One (Is. 6:3).

Paul speaks throughout of marriage as a holy state, as in the admonition: "For this is the will of God, your sanctification: that you abstain from immorality; that each one of you know how to control his own body in holiness and honor, not in the passion of lust like heathens who do not know God" (1 Thess. 4:3-5).[79] What Paul is expressing here is, first of all, the self-awareness of a Jew who is proud of the sexual discipline and order in marriage that prevail in Israel. There is a profound link between the pagans' ignorance of God and their sexual licentiousness. When God is not acknowledged, his creation is abused (Rom. 1:26-27).

In addition, Paul says of Christian marriage that it is a union which sanctifies. Perhaps he is suggesting that it is an intimate personal communion. He seems to be saying that marital cohabitation must be an ever new courting of the woman's love by her husband, so that he may "win" it again. Now, in none of his letters does Paul express so urgently his expectation of the Lord's proximate return as in this First Letter to the Thessalonians (4:13-18). And yet, unlike in the First Letter to the Corinthians, he says nothing about the great blessing of marriage being called into question by this imminent coming. On the contrary, while waiting for the Lord's return, the Christian can and must live holily in marriage.

Especially in 1 Cor. 7 Paul does speak rather meanly of marriage. The Old Testament, the idealist ethics of antiquity, and other parts of the New Testament undoubtedly make other kinds of statements. Yet at the same time we may not charge Paul with, for example, the kind of hostility to the body that was certainly abroad in late antiquity. In his eyes the body and sex are and remain God's creation that has now undergone a new creation. Thus he says: "Do you not know that your bodies are members of Christ? . . . Do you not know that your body is a temple of the Holy Spirit within you? . . . You are not your own; you were bought with a price. So glorify God in your body" (1 Cor. 6:15, 19-20). To live in the body is a way of genuinely worshipping God. "I appeal to you, therefore, brethren, by the mercies of God, to present your bodies as a living sacrifice, holy and acceptable to God, which is your spiritual worship" (Rom. 12:1).

The eternal Son of God, moreover, took to himself a human body, "born of woman, born under the law" (Gal. 4:4). That body was glorified and acquired a new corporeal and spiritual existence in the resurrection and exaltation of Jesus (1 Cor. 15:12-19). Consequently, the hope and promise of a resurrection embrace the whole person, body and spirit.

Paul thinks as a Jew. For him man is not a composite of body and soul, but is a corporeal person, and that person will be restored in the resurrection. How this will happen is a mystery. Everything will be utterly different from what one can imagine (1 Cor.

15:20-53; Phil. 3:21). Christian faith does not contemn the body, but exalts and transfigures it.

4. 1 Corinthians 9:5 (Apostolic Office and Marriage)

Paul turns to those who criticize his service and asks: "Do we not have the right to be accompanied by a sister [a Christian; §12.4] as a wife, as the other apostles and the brethren of the Lord and Cephas?" (1 Cor. 9:5). Paul too has the right to act like the other apostles (whether the term refers only to the Twelve as in 1 Cor. 15:5, or to a broader group, as in 2 Cor. 8:23) and to be accompanied on his missionary travels by a wife and to receive support for himself and her from the community. He renounces such a choice, however, because he wants to preach the gospel without payment, so as not to put any obstacle in its way (1 Cor. 9:12, 18; 2 Cor. 11:7) or give his enemies any excuse for claiming that he seeks to enrich himself from his apostolic activity (1 Cor. 9:12; 2 Cor. 11:7).

At the same time, however, marriage and apostolic office are not exclusive of each other. For example, a married couple, Aquila and Prisca, were his highly esteemed fellow workers in the mission at Ephesus and Rome; in fact, according to the Apostle's own testimony, the entire Church owed them a debt of gratitude (Rom. 16:3-4; Acts 18:2-3). Another couple, Philemon and Apphia, used their house for the meetings of the community at Colossae (Philem. 1-2). The Church of the New Testament never thought of making celibacy a law, at least not for specifically chosen groups or states. It could not do so as long as it was convinced, on the one hand, that marriage is instituted by God, and, on the other, that celibacy is a vocation and a gift (1 Cor. 7:7).—The text of 1 Cor. 9:5 was to be altered in the tradition (§7.7).

§ 7. Later Texts

1. Rules for the Household[80]

The New Testament contains a number of *Haustafeln*, or "Rules for Households" (Eph. 5:22-6:9; Col. 3:18-4:1; 1 Tim. 2:8-15; 6:1-2; 1 Pet. 2:13-3:7), which deal with order within the home and with the relations of family and household to the world around them. The lists of rules follow the schemata of Hellenistic and in particular Stoic ethics, as already reflected in Judeo-Greek teaching. Thus Epictetus' disciple says to him: "As a devout man, a philosopher, and a conscientious disciple, I want to know my duties to the gods, my parents, my brothers and sisters, my country, and my friends" (*Discourses* II, 17, 3). This list of topics provides the outline for the household rules.

From the beginning, the New Testament accepts and follows the secular tradition, but it does so in an increasingly independent manner. Thus the Greek catalogues address only the husband and put the preservation of order into his hands, whereas the New Testament also addresses wives, children, and slaves, and thus emphasizes their personal dignity. That dignity was by no means taken for granted in the social structure of the ancient world.

The duty of honoring the gods is replaced, of course, by the exhortation to obey the one true God. As far as the order of the household is concerned, wives are urged to "be subject to your husbands" (Col. 3:18; Eph. 5:22). Such an admonition reflects the order that antiquity felt to be proper in marriage, as expressed, for example, in Plutarch's *Exhortations to Spouses*: "When women submit to their husbands, they are to be praised, but when they seek to dominate they act disgracefully" (142D). According to the New Testament, the submission should be such "as is fitting in the Lord" (Col. 3:18). This phrase indicates both the reason for the submission and the extent of it. Christ the Lord is master even of the Christian household.

A trait peculiar to the New Testament lists is that children are expressly exhorted (Col. 3:20-21; Eph. 6:1-4). This is the result of the commandment in the Decalogue (Ex. 20:12), which is cited in Eph. 6:2. The same original source is also clearly at work in a list given by Philo (*On the Decalogue* 165ff.) in which regulations for numerous situations are derived from the scriptural commandment to honor one's parents.

A further peculiarity of the New Testament lists is that the exhortations are integrated into the general Christian pattern of mutual service: "Be filled with the Spirit. . . . Be subject to one another out of reverence for Christ" (Eph. 5:18-21). Moreover, a wholly new and specifically Christian term makes its appearance in the household rules taken over from secular ethics: "Husbands, *love* your wives" (Col. 3:19; Eph. 5:25, 28, 33). "Love" expresses the idea and embodies the power that are to determine the meaning and shape of marriage for the Christian consciousness and eventually, in a secularized form, for the profane world as well. (Is not altruism in this sphere perhaps the daughter of charity, even though she no longer acknowledges the latter as her mother?)

The New Testament says nothing of eros as the love that brings about the union of the sexes and its fulfillment. The genius of Plato had unforgettably portrayed the nature and power of eros in the discourses of the participants in the *Symposium*. The priestess Diotima (as reported by Socrates) finally explains the nature of eros by the myth of his birth (203B-204A). At a feast of the gods, *Penia* (Poverty) met *Poros* (Acquisition and Riches), the son of Wisdom. As a result of this meeting, Eros (Desire) was begotten. Eros is the movement that arises between the indigent and the valuable. He is the desire for what is lacking, and the longing to obtain what is valuable and to acquire what will complete him, through the self-surrender that is the highest form of fulfillment. The object of eros need not be a person; it may be a thing or an idea; ultimately, it is the primal divine beauty and goodness. What a person in love desires is the intensification of his own fullness of life and being.

In late antiquity and the New Testament period, however, eros was no longer such a noble figure. As child of Aphrodite, he was either almost demonic lust or else playful affection. He appears in the tragedies of Euripides and the writings of Plutarch (§4), to take two examples, as the power that leads to marriage and then brings marriage to its fulfillment.

Christian love is agape, not eros, for it does not covet but gives. Eros will say, "I love you because you are of such a kind (that is, valuable in some way)," but agape says: "I love you simply because you are." Agape is able to give itself because of the riches that have first been given to it.

It is above all this kind of love that must be found in marriage as a form of Christian community. To it apply the words: "forbearing one another and, if one has a complaint against another, forgiving each other. ... And above all these put on love, which binds everything together in perfect harmony" (Col. 3:13-14). In fact, the entire canticle of love in 1 Cor. 13:4-8 must be fulfilled in marriage: "Love is patient and kind; love is not jealous or boastful; it is not arrogant or rude. Love does not insist on its own way; it is not irritable or resentful; it does not rejoice at wrong, but rejoices in the right. Love bears all things, believes all things, hopes all things, endures all things. Love never ends."

2. Ephesians 5:22-33

One lengthy set of rules for households (Eph. 5: 21-6:9) contains a mystical portrayal of love.[81] The motto for the entire section is: "Be subject to one another out of reverence for Christ." With these words every order of precedence among people is abrogated, since the same reverence for Christ is incumbent on all, and on both sexes equally. The bride who is the Church is subject to Christ her Lord, but subjection is compatible with intimate union: "As the church is subject to Christ, so let wives also be subject in everything to their husbands. Husbands, love your wives as

Christ loved the church and gave himself up for her, that he might sanctify her" (vv. 24-26).

Gen. 2:24 is interpreted in this passage as applying to Christ's love for the Church: " 'For this reason a man shall leave his father and mother and be joined to his wife, and the two shall become one [flesh].' This is a great mystery, and I mean with reference to Christ and the Church" (vv. 31-32). The writer of the letter is aware that Gen. 2:24 refers, and is understood as referring, in the first instance, to all marriages among human beings. Even at this level the words are pregnant with mystery.

But the full depth of the mystery is revealed only when the words are applied to the union between Christ and the Church. The letter sees in these words that were spoken at the dawn of creation about the intimate union of man and woman a prophetic prediction of the union of Christ and his Church. Every marriage in the Church recalls this union of Christ and the Church, and this latter union is represented and made visible, and becomes a concrete reality, in the loving union of the spouses. If celibacy is the eschatological sign of the Church's expectation of her Lord, marriage is the already present sign of the union of Christ and the Church as already realized.

In its exhortation the Letter to the Ephesians also uses, of course, the terms that describe the traditional social relationships of marriage. Wives are to "be subject to their husbands" (5:24). The wife must "respect her husband" (5:33). "The husband is the head of the wife as Christ is the head of the church" (5:23). But these various concepts are interpreted and given a deeper meaning by reference to Christ; their inner structure has been renewed. Christ loves the Church as his body, and "even so husbands should love their wives as their own bodies" (5:28).[82] In Eph. 5:22-23, the theology of marriage as part of the theology of creation according to Gen. 1 and 2 is taken to a higher level by a theology of marriage that is part of a theology of redemption in Christ.

The exegetes ask what the sources were for this theology of marriage. The Old Testament uses the image of marriage to describe God's relationship with his people (Hos. 2:4-6; Jer. 2:2; Ezek. 16:14; §2.5). The idea that Christ loves his Church as his bride is implied or even made explicit in such texts as Mk. 2:9; Mt. 25:1-12; Jn. 3:29, in which Christ is portrayed as the heavenly bridegroom of the community. Paul wants to present to Christ a virginal Church (2 Cor. 11:2). In the Apocalypse of John, the Church, as the new Jerusalem, waits like a splendidly adorned bride for her heavenly marriage. It is an undecided question whether conceptions, either ancient or contemporary with the New Testament, of a "sacred marriage" of God with mankind and the world play a role in this imagery.

The words "This is a great mystery" (Eph. 5:32) were translated in the Latin Bible as *Hoc sacramentum magnum est*, "This is a great sacrament." But "sacrament" here means something like "holy event" and not what we understand today by the term.[83] Since the Latin Church used the Latin Bible almost exclusively for about a thousand years, she found implied or expressed in this text the truth that a marriage entered into in the Church has the rank and value of a sacrament. Catholic teaching maintains that God established marriage in paradise and that Christ raised it to the dignity of a sacrament.

Until the high Middle Ages, the Church did not automatically list seven sacraments as we do today; at times the list included more, at times less. In fact, the very concept of a sacrament as a composite of word and sign that by reason of its institution by Christ communicated grace and salvation[84] was itself formed relatively late, and only then could the number of sacraments, in our technical sense, be determined. Accordingly, it was at the Second Council of Lyons in 1274 that the Church officially established the list of seven sacraments (marriage among them). The Council of Trent, in its twenty-fourth session (1563), repeated this teaching and spelled it out in detail. Trent asserts that marriage, when it is a sacrament, communicates the grace of Christ and thereby brings the natural love between the spouses to a higher level of perfection. It is also Catholic teaching that the couple administer the sacrament to each other and receive it from each other; the assisting priest is simply a witness on behalf of the Church.

Although this teaching on the sacramentality of marriage was formulated only at a late period, it nonetheless has a foundation in the New Testament. The New Testament thinks of Christ as the primordial sacrament, because through word and work he redeemed the world and sanctified, and continues to sanctify, the Church. Marriage in Christ is a sacrament inasmuch as it brings God's love and salvation to bear on the union of the spouses. On the other hand, Eph. 5:32 (in the Greek text) does not speak directly of marriage as a sacrament but of the mystery contained in the words of Gen. 2:24 regarding the Church. Nonetheless, the entire context (Eph. 5:21-33) does state that Christ's love for the Church is represented by, and operative in, marital love. 1 Cor. 7:14 says expressly that God's salvation comes to pass in marriage, for it says that marriage sanctifies the spouses. As a redeemed creation, marriage is a form of the Church.

3. The Pastoral Letters

Further important texts on marriage are to be found in the Pastoral Letters.[85] These are regarded today as having been written about the year 100. One of the letters launches a sharp attack on those who "depart from the faith . . . [and] who forbid marriage and enjoin abstinence from foods which God created to be received with thanksgiving by those who believe" (1 Tim. 4:1-3). These erroneous teachings embody currents of thought with which Paul had been forced to come to grips in his First Letter to the Corinthians, at a time when these ideas were first emerging (§6.3).

In the second century, these false doctrines became even more dangerous and drew strong opposition from the Church's teachers. According to these erroneous doctrines, the world was not created by the good God but was the work of an evil, demonic antigod. Consequently, they forbade the use of the things of the world, commanded fasting, and called for abstention from marriage because marriage continued the work of creation. In the apocryphal acts of the apostles, the latter were represented as requiring the abolition of marriage. In the mid-second century, Marcion forbade marriage in his community as a way of protesting against the evil world. Irenaeus tells of false doctrines which claim that "marrying and pro-creating are Satan's work" (*Adversus haereses* I, 24, 2).

The Pastoral Letters resist this denigration and denial of God's creation. They reject a forcibly imposed asceticism that tries to pass itself off as a higher form of morality but is in fact simply an expression of unbelief (1 Tim. 4:3). This same opposition renders intelligible some other exhortations in the Pastoral Letters. For example, "women should adorn themselves modestly and sensibly in seemly apparel. . . . Woman will be saved through bearing children, if she continues in faith and love and holiness, with modesty" (1 Tim. 2:9, 15). This does not mean that a woman may go ahead and wear herself out with bearing children, on the grounds that she will be blessed for it. Rather, the letter is probably saying that the activities of marriage, if done in faith and love, are holy and bring salvation—something that has not always been taught in the Church's moral theology.

The letter also says: "I permit no woman to teach or to have authority over man" (1 Tim. 2:12; see vv. 11-14). According to Jewish custom, women were to be silent in public (§2.8; 1 Cor. 14:24 = §12.5), while submission to the husband was another requirement of the time (Col. 3:18; §7.1). The letter offers us a reason for this prohibition: "Adam was formed first, then Eve; and Adam was not deceived, but the woman was deceived and became a transgressor" (1 Tim. 2: 13-14). The judgment passed on Eve has clearly become harsher, as it already had in Judaism (§1.5).

The letter here deduces the subordination of woman from the fact that Eve was created after Adam, but this is not the point of the creation story, which says rather that man and woman were created to form a community in which both have the same rights and dignity. The letter accuses Eve, but makes no mention of Adam's sin and fall. Here again, as in connection with 2 Cor. 11:3 (§6.2), the commentators ask whether the Jewish tradition that the serpent seduced Eve into unchastity has exerted any influence. In view of the fact that the biblical story of the origins of mankind has been cited in foregoing verses, the harsh saying that "woman will be saved through bearing children" (1 Tim. 2:15) probably derives ultimately from Gen. 3:17.

In the ideals they propose for various offices, the Pastoral Letters require that bishop, presbyter, and deacon be "the husband of one wife" (1 Tim. 3:2, 12; Tit. 1:6). These texts may be interpreted as meaning that those entrusted with an office must not have been guilty of adultery or an illicit relationship, but they may also be taken to mean that men who have been married more than once may not be admitted to office in the Church—that is, either no new marriage after a legal dissolution of a first marriage, or no new marriage after the death of the first wife.

The Fathers of the Church adopted this second interpretation, and Catholic exegetes especially followed it later on. In this view, the texts would be imposing on officeholders an ascetical requirement regarding marriage, and this in turn could be regarded as the first step toward the latter law of complete priestly celibacy.

Exegetes today, on the other hand, are gradually tending to favor the first of the two interpretations given. Admittedly, it may astound us that bishops and other officials could be suspected as having possibly been guilty of such serious offenses as adultery. And yet other gross failings are also listed: a bishop must not be a drunkard or a man of violence or a lover of money (1 Tim. 3:3).

In any case, the catalogue of vices reflects current lists, and no concrete references need be inferred. In 1 Tim. 3:4, 12, the only positive requirements expressed are that the bishop and the deacon must manage their own households well and raise their children properly. This seems to presuppose that these men lived a life like other people. Moreover, the Pastoral Letters reject the excessive ascetical demands of the heretics. Would they at the same time require a special asceticism from officeholders? No, the texts are in all probability demanding only that officials live a properly ordered married life.[86]

The New Testament Church developed the special class of widows.[87] Biblical and extrabiblical writings alike bemoan the lot of the widow who has been left behind. Widows received support from the Church (Acts 6:1; 9:39; Jas. 1:27). But as united into a class in the Church they also exercised certain functions. The intention of the Pastoral Letters is to bring order into this situation (1 Tim. 5:3-16). The women who make up the class of widows in the Church are to be over sixty years of age and have to be formally enrolled (5:9). Only women really left isolated belong to the class (5:4-5), and not those who are cared for by their families (5:4, 8) or have other means of support (5:16). They must have given evidence of piety (5:5) and good works (5:10). Those to be officially recognized as widows must have been married only once (5:9). The services they render the community are those of assistance and relief (5:10); in turn, they are supported by the community (5:16). In other words, they are appointed officials.

The positions taken in the letter are very realistic. Thus young widows are not to be admitted into this "professional" class; they must first do their duty to their children and take care of their household (5:4, 16). There is great danger that these young widows "may grow wanton against Christ" and "desire to marry again" (5:11). (Is the implication here that they have bound themselves by vow to be brides of Christ?) They frequently engage in idle activity from house to house (5:13). There are even some who live dissipated lives; they are "dead even while alive" (5:6). Therefore, the letter sums up, "I would have younger widows marry, bear children, rule their households, and give the enemy no occasion to revile us" (5:14). The hostile pagan world round about must be given no cause or occasion for malevolent judgments (the same warning occurs in Tit. 2:5; 1 Pet. 4:4; and earlier, in Rom. 14:16).

In the Church order to be found in Tit. 2:1-10, there is a further admonition to women (2:3-5). In keeping with the pattern followed in the lists of sins, the women, too, are warned against gross failings, such as slander and drunkenness. They are to be "reverent [or: priestly?] in behavior." As teachers of what is good, the older women are to instruct the younger. While this commission to teach need not be taken as referring to a public office, it does suggest that the strict prohibition (in 1 Tim. 2:12) against women teaching has at least been softened. Young women, for their part, are to "love their husbands and children, to be sensible, chaste, domestic, kind, and submissive to their husbands."

The life and vocation of woman are thus connected with the home, marriage, and family, and involve subjection to her husband. Greek inscriptions praise the same virtues in women; thus one inscription commemorates "the sweetest of women, one who loved her husband and children." Roman catalogues of virtues require a woman to be *domiseda* ("one who stays at home") and *domum servans* ("one who takes care of her household").

The purpose of all this, says Tit. 2:4, is "that the word of God may not be discredited." The Pastoral Letters repeatedly recommend this kind of regard for the environing world, which is not well-disposed toward Christians (Tit. 2:8, 16; 1 Tim. 3:6-7). Such a concern surely springs from missionary considerations. But the desire to mark the distance from the teaching and pretensions of the gnostics or, in other words, the determination to preserve authentic tradition may also play a role.

In the Pastoral Letters, a Church order regulates the everyday life of Christians. The idea of eschatological existence and the spirituality of the Pauline letters belong to the distant past. For Paul, celibacy is the ideal (1 Cor. 7:1, 8, 26; §6.3), whereas in the Pastoral Letters marriage and numerous children are unquestioningly accepted as the right way of life in the Church. Paul wants widows to remain unmarried (1 Cor. 7:39-40), but the Pastoral Letters decree that at least the younger widows should remarry (1 Tim. 5:14).

4. Hebrews 13:4

The Letter to the Hebrews closes with a number of exhortatory maxims (13:1-6) urging the reader to fraternal love and hospitality, care of prisoners and the ill-treated, and contentment without greed. The passage also contains this exhortation: "Let marriage be held in honor among all, and let the marriage bed be undefiled; for God will judge the immoral and adulterous" (13:4).

The letter seems to presuppose a well-to-do community, but also one that is tempted to adopt a worldly outlook. "Let marriage be held in honor." It is possible to hear in these words, as the Fathers of the Church did in their day, respect for marriage and a defense of it against the doctrines of, for example, gnostic dualism (1 Tim. 4:2; §7.3) or possibly against ascetical tendencies in the Church as well. The Christian holds marriage and the marriage bed in honor and does not think of them as at all unholy. The letter, in fact, applies the same language to Christ the high priest: he is "holy, blameless, unstained" (7:26).

The honor of marriage is violated by immorality

and adultery. In maintaining this conviction, the community is aware that it stands in opposition to the Jews and pagans around it. The latter, too, it may be, forbid adultery as an intrusion into another's marriage and an injury to one's own. Christian morality goes further and rejects extramarital sexual relations as immoral. Such relations were accepted by public opinion in the Greco-Roman world (§4) and by conventional Old Testamental and Jewish thinking (§2.2) as the right at least of the husband. The letter stands in contrast to Judaism when it characterizes Esau as "immoral" and "unclean" (12:6).

5. 1 Peter 3:1-7

The order proper to marriage is again introduced among the rules for households in 1 Pet. 3:1-7. "Likewise you wives, be submissive to your husbands, so that some, though they do not obey the word, may be won without a word by the behavior of their wives, when they see your reverent and chaste behavior" (3: 1-2). Like 1 Cor. 7:12-16, the letter here assumes that it must deal with mixed marriages and that (as was usually the case, in all probability) the Christian party is the wife. In such a household the wife has to be a missionary. The husband may not hear the sermons in church, but he is at least to be won over by the kind of life his wife leads, without any words being spoken. Her reverence for God is to be manifested by her friendly and peaceful spirit. The husband is to sense and perceive that a higher power rules in his wife's life, a power she shrinks from offending and endeavors to obey (3:2, 4). In this way, he will experience the reality of God.

The rules for the households urge the wife to submission; in this they are in agreement with secular texts, as are Col. 3:18 and Eph. 5:24 (§7.1). The exhortation is based on Scripture and the example of the holy women of Israel, who obeyed their husbands; thus Sarah called her husband "lord" (3:5-6; §2.3.1). As Israelite men consider themselves to be sons of Abraham, and Christian men consider themselves to be the descendants of Abraham (Gal. 3:7, 29), so Christian women are to be regarded especially as the daughters of Sarah (3:6).

While the wife is to be subject to her husband, she also enjoys freedom and rights. She is to "let nothing terrify" her (3:6, citing Prov. 3:25). In a mixed marriage this perhaps means that she is not to let herself be pressured into, for example, leaving the Christian community and abandoning the faith. The fear that should motivate a woman is not fear of her husband but fear of God (2:7; 3:5).

Biblical and extrabiblical motivations alike are brought to bear when the letter exhorts women to reflect that "the hidden person of the heart" (3:4) is more precious than artful coiffures, gold ornaments, and expensive clothes. Is. 3:18-24 had long ago castigated the luxurious ways of women in the wealthy culture of the cities. Greek philosophers, especially the Stoics, did the same.[88] A quite similar admonition appears in 1 Tim. 4:19. These texts presuppose that some wealthy women belonged to the community.

The exhortation to husbands is briefer (3:7), but such an exhortation is in any event quite unusual in the rules for households. The wife must be submissive to her husband, but this does not mean that she is at the mercy of his whims. The husband must not forget that women are the weaker sex, and he must on this account show understanding and consideration. His Christian faith should likewise move him to be loving in his behavior toward his wife. Women are "joint heirs of the grace of life" along with their husbands; husband and wife have the same vocation and hope, the same dignity, the same rights. The husband does not have to give commands, but must "bestow honor" on his wife. The letter's final admonition to spouses is: "Let your prayers not be in vain." Shared prayer is the deepest manifestation of loving communion. The marital love of the spouses should have its roots in a common love of God.

6. Revelation 14:3-4

The New Testament found itself forced to defend the dignity and holiness of marriage against any depreciation of it. Has such a depreciation found its way into the New Testament itself, when the Book of Revelation says: "No one could learn that song except the hundred and forty-four thousand who had been redeemed from the earth. It is these who have not defiled themselves with women, for they are virgins" (14:3-4)?

As the words seemingly require, these verses are understood at times to mean that the redeemed are those who, because of the distress the final days bring, have renounced marriage (in accordance with Mt.

19:12 and 1 Cor. 7:26). Are the verses saying, then, that marriage involves "defiling oneself with women"? But such a dismissal of marriage would contradict the entire Bible! Moreover, according to Rev. 7:2-8, the hundred and forty-four thousand represent all the Israelites who have been sealed, that is, the entire redeemed Church, and the latter is not made up solely of celibates. Rev. 14:4 must therefore have a different meaning.

In both the Old Testament (Hos. 2:14-21; Jer. 2: 2-6; §2.3) and the New (Mt. 12:38; Jas. 4:4; Rev. 14:8; 17:2; 18:3), unchastity and prostitution signify apostasy from God and worship of idols; the latter, in fact, was often enough accompanied by ritual prostitution and other kinds of unchastity. The hundred and forty-four thousand of Rev. 14:4 are therefore the believers who have remained faithful to God. In the same vein, Paul describes the Church as the virginal bride of Christ (2 Cor. 11:2).[89]

7. Changes in the Text

The later history of the Church shows that the conflict regarding marriage which had begun in the New Testament was continued. In the course of it, the idea that marriage was something evil and defiling undeniably encumbered the outlook and teaching of theologians at times (§1.4). The history of the text of the New Testament is clear evidence of the danger, for here and there readings crept into the manuscripts which show that people were unwilling to let the text stand and wanted to change the New Testament teaching on marriage.

In Luke 2:36 it is said that the pious widow Anna who greeted the child Jesus in the Temple had, after being a virgin, lived with her husband for seven years and was now an aged widow. Some texts have it that she lived seven days with her husband. Evidently it was thought desirable to make the period of this pious woman's married life as short as possible. In 1 Cor. 7:3 Paul says: "The husband should fulfill his conjugal obligations toward his wife, the wife hers toward her husband" (NAB). Some texts read: "Man and wife should show benevolence toward each other." In 1 Cor. 9:5 Paul asks whether he alone does not have the right, as an apostle, to be accompanied by a sister (a Christian woman: §12.4) as his wife. Not a few manuscripts read: Have I lost the right to take a woman with me as a sister? That is, the Apostle would be living with this woman, not in marriage, but in a brother-sister relationship. In 1 Pet. 3:7 the text says that husbands should "live considerately" with their wives, or, more literally, "live according to knowledge" with them. The word "knowledge" in the Greek text could, however, be taken as a reference to marital intercourse, and it was surely for this reason that some manuscripts read simply: men should live together with their wives.

The earliest New Testament communities generously acknowledge the vocation, dignity, and rights of women in the Church. Was there a retreat along this front as early as the latter part of the New Testament (to be seen, for example, in the addition of 1 Cor. 14:34-35 and in the Pastoral Letters)? It can hardly be denied that such a change did occur in the subsequent history of the Church. In an article illustrated by numerous references, K. Thraede ends by saying that the evidence shows, by and large, "the victory of a hostility against sex that was approved by the Church and was linked to the endorsement of male domination in home and community. This decision affected Europe throughout the Middle Ages and into modern times. The conclusion to be drawn from the historical research is rather clear: Such a decision is demonstrably not an essential part of the Christian message."[90]

§ 8. Birth and Motherhood

The pain and joy of childbirth are, for the Bible, a parable of man's experience.[91] In comparisons that are often quite brief, the pains of labor are an image of historical distress (Is. 21:3; 37:3; Jer. 6:24; 22:23; 50:43; Mic. 4:9-10; Ps. 48:7) or, in many cases, of the eschatological judgment (Is. 13:8; Jer. 4:31; 13:21; 30:6; 50:43; Hos. 13:13).

Every birth is painful—this is a puzzling fact and requires an explanation. One is given in Gen. 3:16 in the form of an etiology (§1.3).

Two postexilic passages in the Book of Isaiah bemoan the fact that after the return from exile in Babylon, Israel was a weak people and its numbers insignificant. It hoped for an increase and renewal of its power, but its hope was almost completely disappointed. "We were with child, we writhed, we have as it were brought forth wind. We have wrought no deliverance in the earth, and the inhabitants of the world have not fallen" (Is. 26:18). The other text, however, speaks not only of the pains but also of the joy of birth. The rebirth has proved a marvelous thing: "As soon as Zion was in labor she brought forth her sons. . . . Rejoice with her in joy, all you who mourn over her" (Is. 66:7-11). The formerly barren woman who is now the mother of many children is an image of the fulfillment God grants contrary to all hope (1 Sam. 2:5; Ps. 113:9; Is. 49:20-21; 54:1).

By choosing and blessing Israel, God has become its father. "Is he not your father, who created you, who made you and established you?" (Is. 32:6). Yes, God has begotten Israel: "You were unmindful of the Rock that begot you, and you forgot the God who gave you birth" (Is. 32:18).

The Old Testament contains moving images of maternal love. The inhabitants of Gibeon had applied the law of vendetta to seven of King Saul's sons and grandsons who had been handed over to them, and had hanged them on a crag near the city. The mother of two of these men, Queen Rizpah, guarded the unburied bodies day and night for many months to keep them from being torn by wild beasts, until at last the dead were buried with honor (2 Sam. 21:1-14).

The Second Book of Maccabees describes not only the harrowing martyrdom of seven brothers but also the suffering, fidelity, and love of their mother, who speaks words of encouragement and comfort to her sons and dies last of all (2 Macc. 7:1-42). The praises of the mother, her courage, and her maternal love are

given extensive and rhetorically artistic expression
in the (postcanonical) Fourth Book of Maccabees
(14:11-17:3; 18:6-24).

The New Testament likewise uses the comparison
of childbirth. As in the Old Testament (Pss. 18:6 and
116:3 in the Greek translation), the resurrection can
be described as death's painful labor (Acts 2:24). The
last days and the judgment are also presented under
the image of birthpains (Mk. 13:8; 1 Thess. 5:3). Paul
interprets the present distress as a travail that will
bring forth imminent salvation (Rom. 8:22). The
Apostle himself suffers the pangs of birth for the sake
of his children (Gal. 4:19). To the heavenly Jerusalem,
which is our mother the Church, Paul applies the words
of Is. 54:1: "Rejoice, O barren one that dost not bear;
break forth and shout, thou who are not in travail; for
the desolate hath more children than she who hath a
husband" (Gal. 4:27).

In the Gospel of John, Jesus speaks these tender
words of farewell to his disciples: "When a woman
is in travail she has sorrow, because her hour has come,
but when she is delivered of the child, she no longer
remembers the anguish, for joy that a child is born
into the world" (16:21). The image sheds light on the
present situation of the disciples: the sorrow they
feel now will turn into abiding joy. The disciples are
bemoaning the departure of Jesus, which will consist
of his suffering and dying and his return to the Father,
but they already have grounds for joy because they
will soon see Jesus again after his resurrection, and
they will enjoy permanent communion, in the Spirit,
with the exalted and glorified Christ. The image used

here in the Gospel may be derived from Is. 66:7-12.

In the vision in Rev. 12:1-5, Israel is described as a woman crying out in labor. As the dragon threatens her, she brings forth a son, the Messiah and Ruler of the world, who is caught up to God until the time of his eschatological manifestation.

To the images of the Bible may be added the striking description in the *Hymns* of Qumran (1 QH 3, 7-12).[92] With racking pain that is almost fatal, a woman gives birth to "the Wonder-Counsellor with his heroic might." Opposite her is another woman who "is pregnant with Delusion" and gives birth in anguish. Interpreters disagree on the meaning of the image. Some see in it the establishment of the Qumran community by its teacher; others see the afflicted community of the last days, which will emerge from Qumran; the majority, however—and with good reason, it seems—see in the text the birth of the Messiah from Israel and the fate of the Messiah's mother. The woman opposite is the hostile mother of the Dragon.

In the New Testament the word "birth" is used to describe the new creation of man by grace. This creation has its source in the resurrection of Christ, which itself is new life out of death: "By his great mercy we have been born anew to a living hope through the resurrection of Jesus Christ from the dead" (1 Pet. 1:3). The new life can also be said to have its source in the word of God, which, according to Gen. 1, calls things into being out of nothingness: "You have been born anew, not of perishable seed but of imperishable, through the living and abiding word of God" (1 Pet. 1:23). "Of his own will he brought us forth by the word of truth" (Jas. 1:18). This new birth takes place through baptism; baptism means being born again of water and Spirit (Jn. 3:3-8). It is a bath of regeneration (Tit. 3:3-5), and the newly baptized are "like newborn babes" (1 Pet. 2:2). Believers are God's children, "born of God" (Jn. 1:13; 1 Jn. 3:9; 5:8).

Jewish belief was familiar with the idea of creation by God, but it found alien the idea of birth from God. Words and ideas comparable to those of the New Testament can be found, however, in the mystery religions. Initiation into the mysteries brings a new birth. Thus, of initiation into the mysteries of Isis it is said that "those who are as it were reborn through her solicitude are called by the goddess to follow the life-giving ways of a new salvation" (Apuleius, *Metamorphoses* II, 21, 6). The New Testament may have taken over this kind of religious language.[93]

One of the things that makes the Bible so rich a document is that it is able to describe the primal experience of human birth in so many ways and in such striking language, and that it can make such effective use of the image of birth.

§ 9. Marriage and Children

According to the New Testament, children are the purpose nature has assigned to marriage (§2.3).

The great philosophers of the Greek world recommended and required strict family planning and even inhuman forms of human breeding. In Plato's ideal state (*Republic* 460E–461C), in order that the offspring may be as healthy and strong as possible, women are to bear children for the state during their best years, that is, from twenty to forty, while men may beget children until they are fifty-five. If these conditions are not met, any child that may be conceived "shall not be brought to light; if this cannot be prevented, it is to be understood that such a child is not to be raised." According to Aristotle (*Politics*, 1335B), the state is to determine the number of children. Any above this number are to be aborted "before the embryo reaches the stage of sensation and life."

The Roman jurists taught that an unborn child is "part of the mother's entrails"; it is not yet a human being and therefore has no rights. Abortion, consequently, was not punishable by law. Allusions in the writers show that in imperial Rome abortion was widely practiced without scruple.

The Stoic philosophers, however, did not agree with these views (§4). The physicians also had a different outlook, since the medical profession was bound by the oath that goes back to Hippocrates: "I will not provide any woman with the means of abortion."[94]

The Old Testament speaks on one occasion of indeliberate abortion; "When men strive together, and hurt a woman with child, so that there is a miscarriage, and yet no harm follows, the one who hurt her shall be fined. . . . If any harm follows [to the woman], then you shall give life for life . . ." (Ex. 21:22–23).

In other words, the woman's life is to be protected; there is no consideration of the child's life. The Greek translation of the Old Testament (third century B.C.) reads as follows: "If the fruit of the womb is not yet formed, the perpetrator shall pay a fine. . . . But if the fruit is already formed, he shall give a life for a life." Greek ethics and medicine are behind this distinction between the unformed and the formed embryo.[95] In this view, the slaying of a viable fetus is murder and must be expiated by death. In contrast to the pagan world around it, Judaism unconditionally rejected any killing of the fruit of the womb. Thus Tacitus notes: "The Jews regard it as a crime to kill an unborn child" (*Histories* V, 5, 6). Respect for life as God's creation and for fertility as a divine blessing (Gen. 1:28) represents one of Israel's deepest convictions.

The New Testament does not touch on these questions, but the Greek world in which Christians found themselves soon forced them to raise them.[96] The first moral treatise produced in the Church, the *Teaching of the Twelve Apostles* (ca. 100 A.D.), contains the following principles: "You shall not destroy the fruit of the womb nor kill the newborn child" (2, 2); "Killers of children and those who destroy the image of God [in the womb] . . . are walking in the way of death" (5, 2). From this point on, the Fathers of the Church repeat the prohibition against abortion.

During this period, the medical doctors of late antiquity considered the case in which the child in the womb was a danger to the mother's life, and they allowed that in extreme cases the child might be killed (in other words, they acknowledged "medical indications"). The Fathers too had no choice but to accept this medical practice. Thus, in response to pagan accusations, Tertullian declares that Christians reject any kind of abortion: "Since homicide is forbidden, we may not destroy the child in the womb. . . . That which will become a human being is already a human being. For every fruit is already contained in its seed" (*Apologeticum* 9, 8). And yet he is forced to grant that "with a cruelty which is unavoidable, the child still in the womb is killed if a transverse presentation prevents birth. For unless it dies, it will kill its mother" (*De anima* 25, 4-5). (Given the medical knowledge of his day, Tertullian here shows a detailed acquaintance with ancient doctoring and its carefully fashioned surgical instruments.) Augustine, probably following the lead of Tertullian, speaks of "fetuses that are cut into pieces and removed from the bodies of pregnant women, lest, if they be left dead in the womb, they may kill their mothers as well" (*Enchiridion* 23, 86). Augustine too accepts harsh necessity.

The Mandean religion condemned the killing of children. Women who killed their children would be punished in the lower world.[97]

Given the realities of everyday life in our time, ethicists, doctors, and jurists are being forced to deal more fully with questions of abortion.[98] The official teaching of the Church rejects the killing of the child in the womb, even in cases where the doctors judge that the sacrifice of the child's life, and this alone, can at least save the mother's life. This is the doctrine contained in the decrees of the Holy Office from 1884 on,[99] in the encyclical letter *Casti connubii* of Pius XI (December 31, 1930),[100] in the addresses of Pius XII on October 29 and November 27, 1951,[101] and most recently in the *Declaration on Some Questions of Sexual Ethics* issued by the Sacred Congregation for the Doctrine of the Faith on January 15, 1976.[102] Both the encyclical of Pius XI and the recent Declaration state that the lives of child and mother alike are sacred and that there can be no "objective reason" that would justify the "direct killing" of a living person.

III

Women in the Community of Disciples and the Church

In our society women have the same rights and opportunities as men, at least in principle, if not yet in practice. Women complain, however, that this is still far from being true in the Church.[103] Will the Church, perhaps after some delay, adapt to the new situation? Is a genuine equality of rights at all possible so long as the office of priesthood is reserved to males?

§ 10. Jesus and Women

In the time of Jesus, a woman's life in Israel was confined almost entirely to family and home. A respectable woman could hardly go out in public (§2.8).

In contrast to these conditions of the day, the New Testament reflects once again a "new creation." Jesus says that he wants to restore the ideal order of creation as intended by God (Mk. 10:6-9). In his own dealings with women, he did not abide by tradition and its constraints, but broke through these.[104]

He did not indeed call a woman to be among the twelve apostles; this would have been simply impossible in view of the situation in Israel. But this is not the only point to be made about his dealings with women.

1. The Synoptic Gospels

A pious Jew, and especially a rabbi (and Jesus was regarded as a rabbi), thought it unbecoming to greet, much less touch, a woman in public. This is not the tone of the Gospels as they tell us of the women around Jesus. It is evident that he heals women no less than men: Peter's mother-in-law (Mk. 1:29-31), the woman with a flow of blood (Mk. 5:21-34), the daughter of the pagan woman in Syrophoenicia (Mk. 7:24-30). On the Sabbath, Jesus sees a woman who has been bent over for eighteen years (Lk. 13:10-17). He summons the woman and heals her by freeing her from Satan who had bound her. He defends the woman, calling her a "daughter of Abraham," which was a very unusual way to speak of a woman. Israelite men liked to be called "sons of Abraham," but rabbis applied the title "daughter of Abraham" only to the Israelite people as a whole. According to this statement of Jesus, women were members of the people with the same rights as men.

As Jesus preached the gospel of the reign of God, he was accompanied not only by the apostles and disciples but also by "some women who had been healed of evil spirits and infirmities: Mary called Magdalene . . . and Joanna, the wife of Chuza, Herod's steward, and Susanna, and many others who provided for them out of their means" (Lk. 8:1-3). The otherwise unknown names vouch for the historicity of the notice. Were these women members of the community?

Jesus traveled about with disciples like other rabbis, but it was quite unthinkable that a rabbi should associate with women. If, then, these women were disciples of Jesus, he was ignoring the view of public opinion that women were not worthy of religious instruction (§2.8). These female disciples were evidently women of rank and wealth who placed their fortune at the service of the gospel. In retaining these women in his company and accepting the help they gave in gratitude for the healing they had experienced, Jesus was showing them all honor before God and men. Mk. 15:40, 47 likewise tells us of women who were with Jesus in Galilee. When the tradition here again preserves some of their names, it shows how highly they were regarded in the community.

The Gospels of Luke (10:38-42) and John (11: 1-12:2) tell us of Jesus staying in the house of the sisters Martha and Mary in Bethany. In Lk. 10:38-42, Jesus is the teacher of the two sisters, and they take care of him as their guest. Other teachers in Israel thought it a waste of time to instruct a woman, and would not even allow a woman to serve them at table (§2.8). The conversation of Jesus with Mary and Martha in the strikingly detailed and thoughtful story in John's Gospel shows the ties of human affection that united the three and goes on to reveal Jesus as the resurrection and the life (11:20-40).

A few days before his death Jesus was effusively honored by a woman; he allowed her to proceed and praised her (Mk. 14:3-9). The Jewish mind must have found it very difficult to accept the fact that Jesus welcomed even women regarded as sinners by the public and promised them the salvation intended for the upright (Lk. 7:36-50; Jn. 7:53-8:11; §4.4).

In both the Gospel and the Acts of the Apostles (§11), Luke makes conspicuous mention of many women. In the material proper to Luke, we already find the anointing by the sinful woman (7:36-53), the visit to Martha and Mary (10:38-42), and the healing of the woman bent over (13:10-17). Other women are the widow of Naim (7:11-17), the woman who praises Jesus' mother (11:27-28), and the women on the way of the cross (23:27-32), as well as the women in the infancy narrative: Mary, Elizabeth (1:24-25, 39-62), Anna (2:36-39). Then there are two parables that Luke alone has preserved: the lost coin (15:8-10) and the unjust judge (18:1-8). Luke alone mentions the saying of Jesus in praise of the widow of Zarephath, to whom Elijah had been sent (4:26).

There was evidently a rich tradition regarding Jesus' association with women. It was on this that Luke drew, and he may well not have exhausted it. Our overall conclusion is that Jesus disregarded Jewish custom and paid special attention to women.

2. The Gospel of John

The Gospel of John likewise tells of this special attention in the story of Jesus and the Samaritan woman (4:1-42). The disciples had gone into the city to buy food. When they returned, "they marveled that he was talking with a woman" (4:27). They were surprised because teachers in Israel certainly did not talk with women. Christ, on the other hand, addressed his word and his summons to men and women alike as he chose.

The evangelist has written an artistic and profoundly meaningful story in which, in a conversation whose successive phases lead ever deeper into the subject, Jesus gives this alien woman lofty revelations about messianic expectation and fulfillment and finally about his own messiahship. The Samaritan woman then hurries into the city and says to people there: "Come and see whether this is not the Messiah." Many believe in him, initially because of the woman's testimony, but then in response to the words of Jesus himself, who stays among them for two days. The woman becomes a mediator, establishing a link with Jesus for those who are willing to listen. The historical character of the story may be questionable, but this does not invalidate what it says about women in the company and community of Jesus.

The story of Easter (Mt. 28:1-10) reports that on Easter morning women were the first to find the tomb empty, meet the risen Lord, and bring news of the resurrection to the disciples. They were the first witnesses to the Easter faith, and as long as the Gospel of Easter continues to be preached, they will be the Church's witnesses to it. According to Jewish law, a woman could not be a public witness. Does Paul have this principle in mind when he makes no mention of the women among the witnesses to Jesus' resurrection (1 Cor. 15:5-8)?

Jesus' conversations with women, especially in the Gospel of John, raise some important questions of literary mode and historicity. In addition to the New Testament Gospels, we have the apocryphal gnostic gospels, and in these Jesus likewise carries on long revelatory conversations with the apostles and the holy women, his mother Mary, and the sisters Martha and Mary (Magdalene). Some of these texts have long been known, for example, the *Pistis Sophia* and the two *Books of Ieû*; others have come to light only recently in the Coptic manuscripts of Nag Hammadi, for example, the *Sophia of Jesus Christ* and the *Dialogue of the Savior*. These writings represent continuations of the New Testament insofar as both sources rightly recognize and give expression to the fact that in Christ a new relationship to women begins, and with this new relationship a dialogue with them. People are correct in saying that women have a special gift for religion. The purpose of the dialogue is precisely to liberate this gift and acknowledge its rights.

3. Women as Apostles

In their exegesis, some of the Fathers bestow the honorary title of apostle on women in the Gospel. Thus, the Samaritan woman whom Jesus met at Jacob's well became the apostle of the city of Shechem. Origen says of her: "Christ sends this woman as an apostle to the inhabitants of the city, for he sets her on fire with his words." And he continues: "Here a woman proclaims Christ to the Samaritans. At the end of the Gospels a woman even tells the apostles of the Lord's resurrection, for she is the first to see him."[105] Theophylact explains: The Samaritan woman "became an apostle after receiving priestly consecration from the faith that had laid hold of her heart. She taught the entire city."[106]

The women who on Easter morning told the apostles about the resurrection are extolled as apostles to the apostles. Hippolytus says: Christ met the women and by his words sent them out; "Eve becomes an apostle; women become God's apostles."[107] Augustine repeats the same idea: "The Holy Spirit made Magdalene an apostle to the apostles."[108] And Bernard of Clairvaux says of the women on Easter morning: "They are sent by the angel to do the work of an evangelist. They become apostles to the apostles as they hasten in the early dawn to proclaim the Lord's salvation."[109]

§ 11. The Acts of the Apostles

1. Peter's Sermon on Pentecost

The Acts of the Apostles gives us a description of the primitive community as it awaited the outpouring of the Spirit: "All these [the apostles] with one accord devoted themselves to prayer, together with the women and Mary the mother of Jesus, and with his brethren" (2:14). Mary is there in the midst of the praying Church. It is a Church in which women have equal rights (as they did not in the synagogue).

Peter the Apostle interprets the event of Pentecost with the help of the prophet Joel's words (2:28-29): "I will pour out my Spirit upon all flesh, and your sons and your daughters shall prophesy . . . and on my manservants and my maidservants in those days I will pour out my Spirit, and they shall prophesy" (Acts 2:17-18). Men and women alike will be filled with the Spirit. Both alike will be called to prophetic proclamation in the Church. The prophet had a vision of the ideal Israel that would come into existence in the age of messianic salvation, a different Israel from that of the old covenant, the Israel known to history, even in the period of the prophets. Then, a few individuals had occasionally been gifted with the Spirit; now, everyone will receive the Spirit of God. Until now, women had to stay in the background; it is characteristic of the new, messianic covenant that men and women have the same vocation in the Church.

2. Some Names

The Acts of the Apostles (5:14; 8:12; 17:4, 12) notes that (many) women joined the community. In fact, we are told that Christian women had already suffered martyrdom: "Saul laid waste the church, and entering house after house, he dragged off men and women and committed them to prison" (8:3). Paul himself tells us (Acts 22:4; 26:10) that some of the imprisoned "saints" were put to death.

Acts also preserves the names of women in the earliest community of disciples. Tabitha was a "disciple" in the city of Joppa (Acts 9:36-43); she is the only woman in the New Testament to be described as a "disciple." "She was full of good works and acts of charity" (v. 36). Israelites too, of course, performed many good works, as their Bible frequently and urgently exhorted them. According to Is. 58:7, authentic worship requires men "to share your bread with the hungry, and bring the homeless poor into your house; when you see the naked, to cover him, and not to hide yourself from your own flesh." As a Jewish girl, Tabitha had probably learned to do good to others and had found joy in it. As a disciple of Christ, she had done the same, in accordance with his word and example. When Tabitha died, the disciples asked Peter to come and give them pastoral encouragement. They brought him to the upper room where Tabitha was laid out. "All the widows stood beside him weeping, and showing coats and garments which Dorcas [= Tabitha] made while she was with them." Peter then remained alone to pray beside the dead woman. Then he cried, "Tabitha, arise!" She sat up, and Peter presented her to the saints. Tabitha is an example of the early Christian woman who helped others out of love.

We today may ask whether the miracle represents a historical fact. The New Testament community believed that the God who will raise the dead at the end of time can now give a sign of that coming resurrection.

Acts 16:13-15, 40 tells of another Christian woman, Lydia. After hesitating and finally being called in the night by a vision of a Macedonian, Paul had crossed from Asia Minor to Europe. The first city in which he and his companions stayed was Philippi, where on the Sabbath they went outside the city to the place in which the Jews were accustomed to pray. There were some women there, among them Lydia, a dealer in purple goods; she hailed from Thyatira, a city famous for its purple dye-works. Purple garments were very expensive, and Lydia was a competent, independent businesswoman. She was also a "God-fearer," as proselytes were called who accepted Judaism's lofty belief in God without binding themselves to the observance of the entire Jewish law. "The Lord opened her heart to give heed to what was said by Paul." After she and her household had been baptized, "she besought" Paul and his companions to stay in her house.

After a not very lengthy period of preaching, the missionaries were jailed. When released, they returned to Lydia's house, where they met the brethren, and then said good-bye and left the city. Lydia worked as an apostle and won her household to the Christian faith. Her home may be regarded as the first Christian "house of God" or church in Europe. Paul kept up an especially cordial relationship with the community at Philippi, as his letter to them shows. He speaks of its members as "my joy and crown" (Phil. 4:1); from them alone he accepted gifts for himself (Phil. 4:4-15; 2 Cor. 11:8-9). We may well think that Lydia too, and indeed Lydia in particular, helped to create this relationship.

Acts tells us, too, that on a journey Paul came to the city of Caesarea on the coast, and while there stayed in the home of Philip "the evangelist." The latter had four unmarried daughters who were prophetesses. As an evangelist, Philip, who himself possessed charismatic gifts (Eph. 4:11), preached the gospel, while his daughters were prophetesses of the new covenant. It should be said in this context that the gift of prophecy was bestowed on virgins consecrated to God. These women lived by God's word and taught it in the community. No one had as yet any idea of the later prohibitions against women as teachers (1 Cor. 14:34 [post-Pauline]; 1 Tim. 2:12; §12.5; §13).

Both Acts (18:1-9) and Paul's letters make highly respectful mention of a Jewish-Christian couple, Aquila and Prisca (Priscilla). Aquila was a well-to-do businessman in the leather trade. It is worth noting that Prisca is often mentioned before Aquila (Acts 18:8, 26; Rom. 16:3; 2 Tim. 4:19). Was she the more important of the two? The New Testament speaks of Aquila in connection with Rome, Corinth, and Ephesus; he was evidently an international trader. Paul got to know the couple during his stay in Corinth (Acts 18:2), where the community used to gather in their home (1 Cor. 16:19). Paul entered Aquila's firm, for he thought it necessary to earn his own living if he was to preserve his freedom. Subsequently he traveled with Aquila and Prisca to Ephesus, where, on this occasion, he stayed only a short time (Acts 18:18-19).

After Paul had left Ephesus (for Jerusalem), a man named Apollos came there. He was a learned Jewish Scripture scholar who had now become a Christian. He preached in the synagogues, where Aquila and Prisca heard him. They "took him and expounded to him the word of God more accurately" (Acts 18: 24-26). Prisca was an experienced and prudent woman and, in addition, gifted as a theologian. She instructed Apollos, himself a trained theologian, and convinced him of her conception of the gospel and the faith.

3. House Communities

From the beginning, the Christian communities used to gather as "house churches," that is, communities that had private homes for their meeting places (Acts 2:46; 18:7; 20:8, 20).[110] In this context, the women of the house are mentioned time and again. Thus Acts reports that the community of Jerusalem used to gather for prayer in the home of Mary, the mother of John Mark. It was there that Peter went after being freed from prison. At Philippi, Lydia, the prosperous dealer in purple goods, received Paul and his companions into her home after she and her household had been baptized. It was there that the community gathered after Paul had been released from prison and wished to say farewell before continuing his journey (Acts 16:4, 40).

In the Letter to Philemon (v. 2), Paul greets the

community in the house of "Apphia our sister." Here a Christian woman, probably Philemon's wife, is addressed as "sister." In this letter Paul asks Philemon to welcome back his runaway slave, Onesimus. Since the slave belonged to the household, Philemon's wife had to share in the decision. In addition, she would also share in his concern for the Christian community that gathered in their home.

The Letter to the Colossians carries greetings to a neighboring community as well: "Give my greetings to the brethren at Laodicea, and to Nympha and the church in her house" (4:15). That is how the text reads in the older tradition. A more recent reading has "Nymphas and the church in his house." The older reading is probably the original and was changed presumably because it seemed strange that a woman should be named as head of the community. The community at Corinth (1 Cor. 14:34-35) and at Rome (Rom. 16:5) gathered in the house of Aquila and Prisca. In the Letter to the Romans, Paul also greets the saints who are with Philologus and Julia, Nereus and his sister, and Olympas (16:15).

Inscriptions and other notices from the ancient world that have been confirmed by excavations tell us of house communities and cult communities in the pagan religions and of Jewish synagogues that were located in private homes. In these, too, women played a significant role. They helped take care of the worship and caritative services that were carried on in their homes and in the community.

§ 12. The Letters of Paul

1. Romans 16:1-16 (Helper; Deaconesses)

The entire corpus of Paul the Apostle's letters shows how highly the Church in its earliest years appreciated the service provided by women. This appreciation finds its clearest expression in the list of greetings in the final chapter of the Letter to the Romans (16:1-16). Paul first names a woman: "I commend to you our sister Phoebe, a deaconess of the church at Cenchreae" (v. 1). Paul is writing this letter to the Romans from Corinth; Cenchreae was Corinth's port city. The Apostle recommends Phoebe to the Christian community at Rome because she will be traveling there. "Receive her in the Lord as befits the saints, and help her in whatever she may require of you, for she has been a helper of many and of myself as well" (v. 2).

Phoebe was evidently a prominent woman in her own secular sphere as well as in the Church. Now she is pursuing her affairs in Rome, and the Christian community there should assist this stranger in every way. This means, first of all, showing her hospitality; then, too, the Romans may have acquaintances and friends who may be able to help Phoebe.

Phoebe also served the church of Corinth in the diaconal office.[111] That is, she shared in the office of those deacons who are mentioned along with the bishops of the church of Philippi (Phil. 1:1) and of the Pastoral Letters (1 Tim. 3:8).[112] Paul goes on to call her a *prostatis*, literally "one (fem.) who stands in front of," whether as protector and helper or as a leader. The term was a title for officials in the clubs and societies of the ancient world.[113]

The category and function of deaconesses underwent further development in the Church. It is indeed likely that 1 Tim. 3:11 is not speaking of deaconesses but simply of the wives of deacons, but on the other hand the text presupposes and says that these wives contributed to the service performed by their husbands. Deaconesses are mentioned in the letter of Pliny (*Epistulae* 96, 8) to the Roman emperor (ca. 112 A.D.) in which he says that statements about the Christian community were elicited under torture from "two slave-women who were called *ministrae* [female servants]."[114] Thus it was known to the pagan public and the courts that there were deaconesses in the Church. In subsequent literature these are frequently mentioned. They form a class comparable to that of widows (§7.3); in fact, at times the widows and the deaconesses were probably identical.

Deaconesses are mentioned after bishops, priests, and deacons as an official ecclesiastical category (Clement of Alexandria, *Paedagogus* III, 97, 2; Origen, *De oratione* 28, 4). The Syriac *Didascalia*, (before 250) describes the hierarchic order of precedence: "The bishop sits for you in God's place; the deacon stands in the place of Christ, and you are to love him; the deaconesses you should honor in the place of the Holy Spirit; the presbyters shall be for you like the apostles, and the widows and orphans you shall consider to be like the altar" (ch. 9).

We have testimonies as far back as the mid-fourth century that deaconesses were appointed to their office by the prayer and laying on of hands of the bishop. Bishop Basil of Caesarea mentions this (*Epistulae* 194, 44), and the solemn rite itself is described in the *Apostolic Constitutions* VIII, 19-20 (ca. 380): at the ordination of deaconesses, the bishop, priests, deacons, and deaconesses lay hands on the future deaconess and invoke the Spirit upon her. This ordination is described between those of the deacon and the subdeacon. As an ordained functionary, the deaconess is here considered to be a member of the clergy.

In the early Byzantine Church, the ordination of the deaconess, like that of the deacon then and today, comprised the laying on of hands, a prayer for the Spirit, and the presentation of stole and chalice. The chief tasks of the deaconess were the pastoral care of women and the caritative works of the community.

Paul next sends greetings to the Christians of Rome, and first of all to Prisca and Aquila as "my fellow workers in Christ Jesus." They have "risked their necks" for Paul, put their lives on the line for him. He thanks them, and with him "all the churches of the Gentiles give thanks" (vv. 3-4). In the further list of twenty-six people to whom Paul sends greetings, eight women are mentioned and singled out for words of praise (vv. 6-13). "Mary, who has worked hard among you." "Tryphaena and Tryphosa"—probably two sisters, which would account for the similar names— "those workers in the Lord." "The beloved Persis, who has worked hard in the Lord." The term "work" or "labor" is often used of the work done in the early Christian mission (Jn. 4:38; Acts 20:35; 1 Cor. 16:16) and in the community (1 Thess. 5:12). These women had an office and ministry in the mission and in the community, in "the work of faith and the labor of love" (1 Thess. 1:3). The mother of Rufus has become Paul's own mother—"his mother and mine" (v. 16). Even Paul, the restless traveler, treasures the concern shown him by a woman.

In the entire epistolary literature of antiquity there is nothing comparable to this list of names in Romans 16. The text reflects the Apostle's pastoral solicitude, which embraces the whole world and yet turns to each person individually and is attentive to him or her.

2. Philippians 4:2-3

In his Letter to the Philippians, Paul mentions Evodia and Syntyche, who "have labored side by side with me in the gospel together with Clement and the rest of my fellow workers" (v. 3). Both women probably had a hand in the establishment of the community. This is why it is a serious matter for Paul to have to admit that they are at odds with one another. He entreats them "to agree in the Lord." Women no less than men were the appointed servants of the gospel and the community.

3. 1 Corinthians 1:11

In his correspondence with the community of Corinth, Paul at one point makes brief mention of a Chloe: "It has been reported to me by Chloe's people that there is quarreling among you, my brethren"

(1 Cor. 1:11). Paul was writing this letter to Corinth while at Ephesus. Chloe was known to the Corinthian community of disciples and was therefore probably a member of it. She must have been an independent and wealthy woman, since she apparently owned a business with employees and traveling agents. But she was also a Christian who recognized her responsibility for the community at Corinth and sent information to Paul. Paul trusts her sense of concern and therefore embarks on an extensive exhortation to unity and peace (1:12-4:21).

4. 1 Corinthians 9:5, etc. (Sisters)

In 1 Corinthians 9:5, Paul asks: "Do we not have a right to be accompanied by a sister as a wife, as the other apostles and the brethren of the Lord and Cephas?" With the help of a special charism (1 Cor. 7:7), Paul lived a celibate life. In addition, he earned his livelihood by the work of his hands (1 Cor. 9:12, 18; Acts 20:34) so that he might be able to preach the gospel without charge. But we cannot make his example in these matters a law for the Church. Along with the apostles, their wives, as fellow workers (6.4), received their upkeep from the community (1 Cor. 9:6; Mt. 10:10).

In the texts we repeatedly find Christian women being called "sisters" (Phoebe in Rom. 16:1; Apphia in Philem. 2; the wives of the apostles in 1 Cor. 9:5). In the pagan world as in the Christian, individuals between whom there were social or religious ties called one another brother. The Jews did the same, since they felt themselves to be one large family (Ex.

2:9; Ps. 50:29; Acts 2:29; etc.), but the title of sister is rare (Jer. 22:18; Song 4:9). The devout at Qumran were deeply conscious of being brothers and forming a brotherhood (1 QS 6, 22; 5, 3-4, 24-26; 10, 25-11, 2; etc.) Christians in turn professed to be brothers and sisters of Christ (Mk. 3:34-35).

Only in the New Testament community, however, do the sisters stand with equal assurance beside the brothers, for the Christian community was already familiar with the words of Jesus: "There is no one who has left house or brothers or sisters or mother or father or children or lands, for my sake and for the gospel, who will not receive a hundredfold now in this time, houses and brothers and sisters and mothers and children and lands, with persecutions, and in the age to come eternal life" (Mk. 10:29-30; see 1 Cor. 7:15; Jas. 2:15, and the texts mentioned just above: Rom. 16:1; Philem. 2; 1 Cor. 9:5). The term "sister" has survived to our own day in a secularized form.

5. 1 Corinthians 11:4-5; 14:33-35 (Prophetesses)

When Paul describes the community's liturgy in First Corinthians, he also mentions the role played by women, saying of them, without distinction, that they "pray and prophesy" in the community (1 Cor. 11:4-5).[115] The terms prayer and prophecy must have the same meaning as applied to men and women. The prayer in question is not only personal and private prayer at home but the celebration of the liturgy with the assembled community. A woman who is a prophetess belongs with the prophets as the charismatic preachers of the Church who are often mentioned in the Acts of the Apostles (11:27; 13:1; 15:32; 21:10-11) and the letters of Paul (1 Cor. 12:28-29; Eph. 3:5; 4:11). Prophecy is one of the most precious of the charisms (1 Cor. 12:10, 28-29), for the prophet "speaks to men for their upbuilding and encouragement and consolation" (1 Cor. 14:3).[116]

The women in the Corinthian community, then, serve "in the pulpit and at the altar." (It is a secondary matter that Paul wants women to wear a veil at the public meetings of the community, in accordance with Jewish custom: 1 Cor. 11:5-16; §6.2.) When Paul says of the assembly: "when you come together, each one has a hymn, a lesson, a revelation, a tongue, or an interpretation" (1 Cor. 14:26), his statement applies equally to men and women.

A little later, indeed, in this same letter to the Corinthians, when speaking about order in the liturgy, Paul says: "As in all the churches of the saints, the women should keep silence in the churches. . . . If there is anything they desire to know, let them ask their husbands at home" (1 Cor. 14:33-35).[117] But these words about women remaining silent in church must not be cited in isolation, as they often are, for 1 Cor. 11:4-5 must also be taken into account. In view of the latter verses, 1 Cor. 14:34-35 is not issuing a general prohibition against women speaking, but requiring at most that women not take part in the discussion of doctrine at the community gatherings.

Even with this limitation, however, it is difficult, although perhaps not impossible, to harmonize the two passages of the letter. Moreover, 14:34-35 seems to betray un-Pauline usage. Thus Paul has twelve formulas for introducing citations from the Old Testament, but only in 14:34 do we find "as even the law says." (Is the reference to Gen. 3:16?) Verses 33b-35 also break the continuity, since verses 32 and 36 are speaking of the prophets in the community. Also to be explained is why verses 34-35 come after verse 40 in some important manuscripts and ancient translations and in the commentary of Ambrosiaster (fourth century). The evidence is increasingly leading exegetes to the conclusion that verses 34-35 were not written by Paul but were added to the text at a later date. They may originally have been a marginal notation in a manuscript, and then have been incorporated into the Pauline text, in some cases after verse 33a, in others after verse 40. The Church of a later period wanted women to keep silent and not preach in the community (1 Tim. 2:12; §13.1). Perhaps the little passage 33b-35 reflects this attitude.

6. Galatians 3:26-28

In the discussion of women's role in the Church, Gal. 3:26-28 is often quoted, and indeed it is a passage whose meaning is almost inexhaustible. It tells us that, because of baptism, in the community of faith "there is no longer Jew nor Greek, there is no longer slave nor free, there is no longer male and female, for you are all one in Christ Jesus" (3:28, literal). The religious distinction between Jews and Greeks, the social distinction between slaves and free men, and the natural distinction between men and women evidently continue as facts of experience. But these distinctions have now become unimportant, since they have no significance as far as salvation in Christ is concerned. This salvation is communicated in a hidden, sacramental manner, and is therefore not a datum of secular experience.

In speaking of the first two pairs of opposites, Paul says: "no longer (this) nor (that)," but when he comes to the third pair he says "no longer (this) and (that)." The difference is surely not without meaning. "Male and female" is a citation from Gen. 1:27; consequently the polarity in this instance is part of the created order. It cannot simply be eliminated, but it is indeed transcended in the new creation of "the children of God" (Gal. 3:26).

In this new creation, the ideal equality of man and woman as intended by the Creator and expressed in Gen. 1:27 is restored after it had disappeared in the sentence inflicted in Gen. 3:16 and even more in subsequent history. The historical inequality no longer exists in principle, since the saving event embraces both equally, and both have the dignity and rights in the community of the redeemed, the Church. From this fact and principle careful reflection can derive the concrete ways in which the freedom and equality of men and women should be recognized in the Church's law.

While we are on Gal. 3:28, we may perhaps also ask whether Paul does not underestimate and curtail the fruitful tension between man and woman that is proper to the created order (for example, in 1 Cor. 7).

§ 13. Later Texts

1. The Pastoral Letters

In these letters of the late apostolic age (§7.3), women are exhorted to simplicity, efficiency, cheerfulness, and good works. It seems that a spirit of fanaticism was making its way into the Church. Perhaps women were among those cultivating it. As was soon to be even more the case in gnosticism, false teachers were attacking the value and dignity of marriage by calling it the work of the flesh or even of the devil.

For this reason, First Timothy gives instructions for community life and the liturgy. According to it, women have in principle the same right to pray as men; like the men, the women should wear festive clothing when they pray. But the writer then goes on to say: "Let a woman learn in silence with all submissiveness. I permit no woman to preach or to have authority over men" (1 Tim. 2:8-12). The Pastoral Letters show us that in the late apostolic period, the service given by women to the Church was being pushed into the background. Had the Jewish tradition once again set limits to Christian freedom?

At the same time, however, the Pastoral Letters also witness to the service of women in the Church. 1 Tim. 3:5-13 gives a detailed description of the office of deacon in the community. In the midst of this passage we read: "The women likewise must be serious, no slanderers, but temperate, faithful in all things" (v. 11). Since the time of the Church Fathers, it has been debated whether the reference is to women deacons or to the wives of the deacons. In the latter case, it is at least being said that these wives share in their husbands' service.

The Pastoral Letters bear witness, moreover, to the formulation of an office and class of widows in the Church (§7.3). This office and class continued to be important and respected in the Church, and they are mentioned repeatedly in the writings of the early period. Meanwhile, other women who were not widows in the strict sense were received into the group.

The *Apostolic Church Order* (ca. 250-300), for example, says: "Three widows are to be appointed. Two shall pray perseveringly for all who are being tempted and for the reception of revelations in time of distress. The third shall take care of women who are afflicted with illness. They are to be zealous and temperate and to communicate to the presbyters the information they ought to have" (ch. 9). Accordingly, the primary task of the widows is to pray for the community, a task already mentioned in 1 Tim. 5:5.

Similarly, the *Testament of Our Lord Jesus Christ* (fifth century) says: "On Sundays a widow shall join the deacons in visiting the sick" (I, 40). Widows, who had themselves experienced the support of the community (§7.3), now provided the same service to others. For this the community esteemed and honored them. During the liturgy they had a place of honor after the bishop and priests. They represented the beginning of that care of the sick in which religious women have given such valuable service to the Church and society. Our modern secular "sisters of the sick" (nurses) are the successors of these women religious.

2. The Apocalypse of John

In the late apostolic period, the letter to the community at Thyatira in Rev. 2 gives us a glimpse of the life and important place of a prophetess in the Church: "I have this against you, that you tolerate the woman Jezebel, who calls herself a prophetess and is teaching and beguiling my servants to practice immorality and to eat food sacrificed to idols" (2:20). The Apocalypse is not finding fault here with the fact that a prophetess has appeared in the community and at the liturgy; the problem is rather that this prophetess, who is influential and has a following, is leading (many) people astray into immorality and idolatry.

Ever since Old Testament times, idolatry could be called "immorality" (§2.3), and this may be the meaning of the word here (as in Rev. 2:14). On the other hand, apostasy into idolatry could in fact easily be accompanied by immorality in the literal sense (1 Cor. 6:12-20). It was not easy for Christians, who were a majority, to assert themselves against the prevailing paganism around them. The Apocalypse accuses the prophetess of causing Christians to apostatize into paganism. Such an apostasy need not have taken any obvious form; the prophetess may simply have been teaching a worldly, adulterated form of Christianity, of the kind the apocalyptic writers characterized as pagan. Perhaps the prophetess represented a gnostic movement that sought deeper "knowledge," since she claimed to give knowledge of "the deep things of Satan" (2:24).

Perhaps a sector of the community did not recognize the danger. Even Paul had difficulty in keeping the Christians of Corinth from sharing in food that had been offered to idols (1 Cor. 8-10). But God, "who searches mind and heart" (2:23), knows what is going on and denounces it. The prophetess is called "Jezebel" after the foreign queen who became King Ahab's wife and tried to force her own idolatry on him and Israel (1 Kg. 16:31).

The Book of Revelation can serve us here as a transition to the second-century heretical movement and church known as Montanism. In this movement prophetesses played an important role and, in the judgment of the Church universal, a dangerous one. The account given by Bishop Epiphanius (*Panarion*, Heresy 49) mentions the prophetesses of a Montanist sect. During the sect's liturgy, seven torch-bearing young women came forward to prophesy; there were women bishops and women priests. This situation was justified by an appeal to Gal. 3:28: "There is no longer male and female." Inevitably, such developments greatly hindered the service of women in the rest of the Church.

§ 14. Offices and Priesthood for Women[118]

In recent years a number of Roman magisterial documents have called for and encouraged the promotion of women's rights. In its Dogmatic Constitution on the Church, the Second Vatican Council insists that "in the Church there is . . . no inequality arising from race or nationality, social conditions or sex, for 'there is neither Jew nor Greek; there is neither slave nor freeman; there is neither male nor female. For you are all "one" in Christ Jesus' (Gal. 3:28)" (no. 32).[119] According to the Pastoral Constitution on the Church in the Modern World, the basis for the equal dignity of all human beings is the fact that man and woman alike are made in the image of God, as we are told in the story of creation. The Council therefore demands that women be given "the chance freely to choose a husband, or a state of life, or to have access to the same educational and cultural benefits as are available to men" (no. 29).[120] The Decree on the Apostolate of Lay People draws the conclusion that "their participation in the various sectors of the Church's apostolate should likewise develop" (no. 9).[121]

In decrees issued by Rome, women have been granted certain liturgical functions. A pontifical commission established to study the place and role of women in Church and society in the light of the Bible came to the conclusion that no argument against the ordination of women could be derived from sacred Scripture.

After an address by Pope Paul VI, a diocesan newspaper of December 19, 1976 reported: "The degradation of women in many areas of society's life today is, according to the words of the Pope, a challenge to the entire Church. The Church must be on the side of women, the Pope stated emphatically to the members of the Italian Women's Center. To some extent, said the Pope, we can understand the often bitter reactions of the various feminist movements to the unjustifiable treatment of women in work situations and in society at large. Their participation in the life of society must not only be recognized but promoted and sincerely valued."[122]

There is perhaps no Church in which the question of priesthood for women is not being discussed today. Some Churches and ecclesial communions have begun to ordain women priests. Catholic canon law, however, maintains that "only a baptized male can be validly ordained" (canon 968). Is this restriction to be found only in later and contemporary law, or does it represent a constitutional law of the Church from its very beginning? Catholic dogmatic theologians seem to have become uncertain about the answer to the question. If the common priesthood of the Church (1 Pet. 2:5; Rev. 1:6)[123] is the basic, foundational priesthood, and if the special office of priesthood simply gives expression in word and action to that universal priesthood, then the question arises: Why must the special office be restricted to males?

It is a fact, of course, that for two thousand years the office of priest as developed in accordance with law has been exercised in the Church only by men. It is under these conditions that it has acquired its form, configuration, and content. It is not possible for women without further ado simply to become participants in an office that has thus been administered and shaped. Both the office and the Church herself would have to accept new ideas and regulations if women too were to become the representatives, in the special office of priesthood, of the common priesthood of the Church. Even before that, there would have to be a great and difficult adjustment over a long period within the community of faith, teaching, and love.

In a Declaration of October 15, 1976, the Roman Congregation for the Doctrine of the Faith responded to the question of ordination for women and to the contemporary discussion of the subject.[124] The Declaration says that when it came to respect and esteem for women, Jesus "acted quite differently from his fellow countrymen and deliberately, indeed boldly, went his own way." Since, however, he did not call a woman to be a member of the college of twelve apostles, the Church must "be faithful to the Lord's example." The Declaration also recognizes that Paul set a high value on the collaboration he received from women in his apostolic work. Yet, according to 1 Cor. 14:34, Paul also forbade women to speak in church, that is, "to exercise the public role of teacher in the Christian community."

In accordance with these facts of Scripture, the Declaration rejects the admission of women to the priesthood. It goes on to argue, in defense of this rejection, that the priest acts in the person of Christ and must therefore be a male. At the same time, however, the Declaration says that the priest also acts in the person of the Church. We may therefore ask whether the Church, being the bride of Christ, could not be represented by a woman. Moreover, the Church has acknowledged the right of women to baptize, at least in case of necessity. In addition, it is the couple, man and woman, who administer the sacrament of matrimony to one another. Thus women are qualified and empowered to administer sacraments.

The joint Synod of the dioceses of the German Federal Republic, in its statement on "Pastoral Services in the Community,"[125] recalls that "women performed numerous important services in the New Testament community" and that "during the first Christian centuries women as well as men were ordained deacons." The Synod also stresses the fact that in many Churches today women "exercise a whole range of functions that in and of themselves are proper to the office of deacon." "The exclusion of women from diaconal ordination represents a division of function from sacramentally communicated authority in the order of salvation, which has no theological or pastoral justification." The Synod therefore recommends that women be admitted to ordination to the diaconal office. At the same time, the Synod notes that because of the historical background, "the question of the admission of women to the sacramental diaconate is different from the question of women as priests."

The Gospels already show that the relation of Christ to the Church is that of spouse to bride (Mk. 2:19; Mt. 25:1-12). This idea is developed and acquires a new profundity in the writings of the apostles. Paul wants to bring the Church to Christ as a virginal bride to her husband (2 Cor. 11:2). The Church, as the heavenly Jerusalem, is "our mother" (Gal. 4:26). The union between Christ and Church is the mysterious realization of the marital love between husband and wife (Eph. 5:31; §7.2). In a vision of the Apocalypse (12:1-6), a wondrous woman appears in the heavens; she is the true Israel, the Church. Another vision describes the splendid marriage of the Lamb with the Church (Rev. 19:7-8; 22:2).

Toward the very end of John's Apocalypse, we find the words: "The Spirit and the Bride say, 'Come!'" (22:17). This is the response to the promise of the exalted Lord: "Behold, I am coming soon" (22:12). The "Spirit" is the Holy Spirit, represented as an independent reality, who is present in the Church. He is understood to be a person, as in other texts that manifest the final stages of New Testament thought (Mt. 28:19; Jn. 15:26; 2 Cor. 13:13). Spirit and Bride both stand for the Church. The Church is a bride as in Rev. 19:7; 21:2, 9 (see 2 Cor. 11:2; Eph. 5:25-26; §7.2). Spirit and Bride make one entity: the Spirit-filled Church, and this Church asks that her Lord come to her: "Come!" Her prayer is also a summons to the world; it is the call of the missionary Church that seeks to bring men to faith and to the Church herself: "Come!" The cry is taken up by the hearers, who in turn say: "Come! Let him who is thirsty come, let him who desires take the water of life without price" (22:17).

The scene represents a liturgy in which the world

is called to salvation through the gospel. In the person
of the bride, the Church issues the call. Now if the
Church can thus be symbolized by a bride, can she
not also be represented in the concrete person of a
woman? Cannot a woman do prophetic and priestly
work in the Church (as she does in 1 Cor. 11:5)?

NOTES

1   On the general theme of women in the Bible, the following
    may be consulted. K. Thraede, "Frau," *RAC* 8 (1972), pp.
    197-269. — C. Bamberg, "Bibel und Frau," *Anima* 19 (1964),
    pp. 304-17. — P. Evdokimov, *Die Frau und das Heil der Welt*
    (Munich, 1960). — M. von Faulhaber, *The Women of the
    Bible*, tr. B. Keogh from 8th German ed., 1938 (Westminster,
    Md., 1955). — P. Grelot, *Man and Wife in Scripture*, tr. R.
    Brennan (New York, 1964). — P. Jordan, *Die Töchter Gottes*
    (Frankfurt, 1973). — F. Heiler, *Die Frau in den Religionen
    der Menschheit* (Berlin, 1977). — P. Ketter, *Christus und die
    Frauen*. 1. *Die Frauen in den Evangelien* (Stuttgart, 1948⁴);
    2. *Die Frauen in der Urkirche* (Stuttgart, 1949). The 2nd ed.
    of Vol. 1 was translated by I. McHugh as *Christ and Woman-
    kind* (London, 1937). — Th. Maertens, *La promotion de la
    femme dans la Bible: Ses applications au mariage et au minis-
    tère* (Tournai, 1967). — E. Moltmann-Wendel (ed.), *Mensch-
    enrechte für die Frau: Christliche Initiativen zur Frau-
    enbefreiung* (Munich-Mainz, 1974). — H. Rusche, *They
    Lived by Faith: Women in the Bible*, tr. E. Williams (Balti-
    more, 1963). — L. Schäppi, "Die Stellung der Frau im Juden-
    tum, im Islam und im Christentum," *Judaica* 32 (1976), pp.
    103-12, 161-72. — E. Schüssler, *Der vergessene Partner*
    (Düsseldorf, 1964). — E. Stein, *Die Frau: Ihre Aufgabe nach
    Natur und Gnade* (Freiburg, 1959).

2   Some of the more important commentaries: H. Junker, *Gene-
    sis* (Echter-Bibel; Würzburg, 1949). — G. von Rad, *Genesis:
    A Commentary*, rev. ed. (1972) tr. J. H. Marks (Philadelphia,
    1972). — C. Westermann, *Genesis 1-11* (Biblischer Kom-
    mentar—Altes Testament; Neukirchen-Vluyn, 1974). — R.

Goeden, *Zur Stellung von Mann und Frau, Ehe und Sexualität im Hinblick auf Bibel und Kirche* (dissertation; Göttingen, 1969). — O. Loretz, *Schöpfung und Mythos* (Stuttgart, 1968). — J. B. Schaller, *Gen 1.2 im antiken Judentum* (typed dissertation; Göttingen, 1961). — J. Scharbert, *Fleisch, Geist und Seele im Pentateuch* (Stuttgart, 1967²). — H. W. Schmidt, *Die Schöpfungsgeschichte der Priesterschrift* (Neukirchen-Vluyn, 1964²). — O. H. Steck, *Die Paradieseserzählung: Eine Auslegung von Genesis 2, 4b-3, 24* (Neukirchen-Vluyn, 1970). — F. J. Stendebach, *Der Mensch . . . wie ihn Israel vor 3000 Jahren sah* (Stuttgart, 1972). — W. Trilling, *Am Anfang schuf Gott* (Leipzig, 1964²). — Idem, *Denn Staub bist du* (Leipzig, 1964). — H. W. Wolff, *Anthropology of the Old Testament*, tr. M. Kohl (Philadelphia, 1974).

3 See my *Theology of the New Testament* 1:3-13.

4 C. Westermann, *Genesis*, pp. 48-52. See V. Maag, "Sumerische und babylonische Mythen von der Erschaffung des Menschen," *Asiatische Studien* 8 (1954), pp. 85-106.

5 Westermann, p. 316.

6 O. Schilling, *Das Mysterium Lunae und die Erschaffung der Frau nach Gen 2, 21* (Paderborn, 1963).

7 The derivation of *ishah* (woman) from *ish* (man) is an etymology based on sound. The philologists cannot further explain *ishah*. See J. Kühlewein, "Frau (issah)," in E. Jenni and C. Westermann (eds.), *Theologisches Handwörterbuch zum Alten Testament* 1 (Munich-Zürich, 1971), pp. 247-51.

8 J. Scharbert.

9 R. A. Batey, "The *MIA SARX* Union of Christ and the Church," *New Testament Studies* 13 (1966-67), pp. 270-81; Th. Boman, *Hebrew Thought Compared with Greek*, tr. J. L. Moreau (London, 1960), pp. 96-97.

10 *Plato: The Symposium*, tr. W. Hamilton (Baltimore, 1951), p. 62.

11 Westermann, pp. 217-18.

12 H. L. Strack and P. Billerbeck, *Kommentar zum Neuen Testament aus Talmud und Midrasch* 2 (1924), p. 373.

13 W. Foerster, "ophis," *TDNT* 5:566-82.

14 K. Elliger, *Leviticus* (Tübingen, 1966), pp. 191-99.

15 C. Jenkins, "Origen on 1 Corinthians," *Journal of Theological*

     Studies 9 (1907-8), pp. 501-2.

16   *Commentarii in Epistulam ad Titum* 1, 8 (*PL* 26:603BC).

17   *Adversus Jovinianum* 1, 20 (*PL* 23:249AB).

18   *De Exodo* (*CCL* 78:501-41); *Epistulae* 49, 15 (*CSEL* 54: 376-78).

19   *Epistulae* 11, 56a, 8. On the statements of the Fathers, see R. Goeden, pp. 138-40 (Origen); 118-22 (Jerome); 191.

       H. V. Wili, "Zur Zölibatspflicht der Weltkleriker im katholischen Kirchenrecht," *Theologische Berichte* 4 (Zürich, 1974), observes: "Harking back to the concept of cultic purity in the Old Testament (Ex. 19:14-15; 1 Sam. 21:5), the West, in consequence of the daily celebration of the Eucharist, developed the requirement of temporary abstinence into a requirement of continual and permanent continence, and probably did so as early as the third century" (p. 191).

20   *Catechismus Concilii Tridentini*, Part II, ch. 2, no. 58, tr. J. A. McHugh and C. J. Callan, *Catechism of the Council of Trent for Parish Priests* (New York, 1934), p. 248.

21   Encyclical letter *Sacra Virginitas* (March 25, 1954), in *AAS* 46 (1954), pp. 169-70; tr. in *The Pope Speaks* 1 (1954), p. 108.

22   *De opificio mundi* 151, 156, and 165.

23   *Ibid.*, 165, tr. F. H. Colson and G. H. Whittaker, *Philo* 1 (Cambridge, 1962), p. 131.

24   A. Oepke, "Ehe," *RAC* 4 (1959), cols. 650-60. — G. Delling, "Eheleben," *RAC* 4 (1959), cols. 691-707. — H. Eising, "Ehe im Alten Testament," in A. Beckel (ed.), *Ehe im Umbruch* (Münster, 1969), pp. 81-105. — J. Hempel, *Das Ethos des Alten Testaments* (Göttingen, 1964), pp. 162-81; 301-16. — H. van Oyen, *Ethik des Alten Testaments* (Gütersloh, 1967), pp. 164-72 (Marriage and Family). — W. Plautz, *Die Frau in Familie und Ehe: Ein Beitrag zum Problem ihrer Stellung im Alten Testament* (typed dissertation; Kiel, 1959). "Monogamie und Polygynie im Alten Testament," *Zeitschrift für die alttestamentliche Wissenschaft* 75 (1963), pp. 3-27. — H. Ringeling, "Die biblische Begründung der Monogamie," *Evangelische Ethik* 10 (1966), pp. 81-102. — R. de Vaux, *Ancient Israel: Its Life and Institutions*, tr. J. McHugh (New York, 1961), pp. 19-61 (Family Institutions).

25   Ancient Eastern collections of laws—Hittite, Assyrian, and

Babylonian—that may have originated in the centuries just before and after 1500 B.C., and thus at around the time of Abraham, show likenesses in form and content to the laws of the Pentateuch. This is true, among others, of laws regarding sex and marriage. In both sets of laws there are comparable prescriptions for marriage and divorce, deliberately procured abortion, incest, homosexual intercourse, and bestiality. Monogamous marriage was probably the usual practice, but the man was allowed plural marriage as well as extramarital relationships. He could at any time dismiss his wife for any reason, but when he did, he had to return the dowry she had brought with her.

The Code of Hammurabi (1728-1686) contains rules that remind us of the relationship between Abraham, Sarah, and Hagar according to Gen. 16 and 21:1-21. A childless wife can give her husband a slave-woman as a secondary wife (no. 145). If she later, after bearing children, sets herself up as the equal of her mistress, she can be reduced to bondage (no. 146). The father can acknowledge the slave-woman's children (no. 170); otherwise these children do not have the same rights as the man's other children (no. 171). The law protects the slave-woman's children if they are driven from the home (no. 172). — The Code of Hammurabi is here cited according to R. Haase, *Die keilschriftlichen Rechtssammlungen in deutscher Übersetzung* (Wiesbaden, 1963). See also H. J. Boecker, *Recht und Gesetz im Alten Testament und im Alten Orient* (Neukirchen-Vluyn, 1976). P. Rémy, "La condition de la femme dans les codes du Proche-Orient ancien et les codes d'Israël," *Sciences ecclésiastiques* 16 (1964), pp. 107-27, 291-320.

26   G. Delling, "Ehebruch," *RAC* 4 (1959), cols. 666-77; F. Hauck, "moicheuō," *TDNT* 4:729-35; F. Hauck and S. Schilz, "pornē," *TDNT* 6:579-95; H. Schüngel-Straumann, *Der Dekalog—Gottes Gebot?* (Stuttgart, 1973), pp. 47-53, 56-61.

27   G. Delling, "Ehescheidung," *RAC* 4 (1959), cols. 707-19; K. Schubert, "Ehescheidung im Judentum zur Zeit Jesu," *Theologische Quartalschrift* 151 (1971), pp. 23-27.

28   Strack-Billerbeck, 1 (1922), pp. 318-19.

29   "It may be said that at this point there was no marriage among Jews that the husband could not dissolve out of hand but in

a fully legal way by giving his wife a bill of divorce" (Strack-Billerbeck, pp. 319-20; see pp. 312-20).

30 *Antiquities of the Jews* XIV, 300; XV, 319; XVII, 14.

31 The story of Michal is given according to the Books of Samuel. These Books also tell of the later tragic events (2 Sam. 6:16-23; also 2 Sam. 21:8, assuming that Michal and Merab are here one and the same). For literary-critical analysis, see "David und Mikal. Überlegungen zur Jugendgeschichte Davids," in J. Hempel and L. Rost (eds.), *Von Ugarit nach Qumran* (Beihefte zur Zeitschrift für die alttestamentliche Wissenschaft 72 [1958], pp. 224-43); *Das erste Buch Samuel* (Gütersloh, 1973), pp. 351-52.

32 W. Bousset and H. Gressmann, *Die Religion des Judentums in späthellenistischer Zeit* (Tübingen, 1966⁴), pp. 425-29.

33 Strack-Billerbeck, 2 (1924), p. 373; 4/1 (1928), p. 30.

34 Strack-Billerbeck, 3 (1926), p. 468.

35 Strack-Billerbeck, 1 (1922), p. 300.

36 H. Strothmann and P. Keseling, "Askese," *RAC* 1 (1950), cols. 749-95.

37 Strack-Billerbeck, 3 (1926), pp. 370-71. See also §1.4.

38 W. Schrage, "Die Stellung zur Welt bei Paulus, Epiktet und in der Apokalyptik," *Zeitschrift für Theologie und Kirche* 61 (1964), pp. 125-54.

39 H. Braun, *Spätjüdisch-häretischer und frühchristlicher Radikalismus* 1 (Tübingen, 1957), pp. 39-41, 131-33; H. Hübner, "Zölibat in Qumran," *New Testament Studies* 17 (1970-71), pp. 153-67; A. Marx, "Les racines du célibat essénien," *Revue de Qumran* 7 (1970-71), pp. 323-42; A. Steiner, "Warum lebten die Essener asketisch?" *Biblische Zeitschrift* N.F. 15 (1971), pp. 1-28.

40 In his *Apology*, as recorded in Eusebius, *Praeparatio evangelica*, VIII, 11, 5.

41 Translated by T. H. Gaster in *The Dead Sea Scriptures* (Garden City, N.Y., 1976³), p. 85.

42 J. Gamberoni, "Das Elterngebot im Alten Testament," *Biblische Zeitschrift* N.F. 8 (1964), pp. 159-60; H. Schüngel-Straumann, pp. 69-72.

43 M. Noth, *Leviticus: A Commentary*, tr. J. E. Anderson (Phila-

delphia, 1962), p. 140; K. Elliger, p. 256. — R. Kilian, *Literar-kritische und formgeschichtliche Untersuchung des Heilig-keitsgesetzes* (Bonn, 1963), p. 36, foregoes any attempt to explain it.

44 Strack-Billerbeck, 1 (1922), pp. 705-11.

45 The task of the women is explained in Ex. 8:8 on the model of the service rendered by the Levites according to Num. 4:23; 8:24. 1 Sam. 2:22 can hardly be explained as evidence of cultic prostitution, although such a practice did exist, according to 1 Kg. 14:24 and 2 Kg. 23:7. 1 Sam. 2:22 "represents rather an addition from the theological thinking of a later time when sin was increasingly identified with sexual sin" (H. J. Stoebe, *Das erste Buch Samuel,* pp. 114-15).

46 Strack-Billerbeck, 4/2 (1928), pp. 45-46.

47 See 1 Thess. 2:15 and my *Theology of the New Testament* 4:180ff.

48 E. Burck, *Die Frau in der griechisch-römischen Antike* (Munich, 1969). — H. Cancik-Lindemaier, "Ehe und Liebe: Entwürfe griechischer Philosophen und römischer Dichter," in H. Cancik-Lindemaier *et al., Zum Thema Frau in Kirche und Gesellschaft* (Stuttgart, 1972), pp. 47-80. — K. Gaiser, *Für und wider die Ehe: Antike Stimmen zu einer offenen Frage* (Munich, 1924). — A. Lesky, *Vom Eros der Hellenen* (Göttingen, 1976). — J. Vogt, *Von der Gleichwertigkeit der Geschlechter in der bürgerlichen Gesellschaft der Griechen* (Mainz, 1960). — E. Zinn, "Erotik," in *Lexikon der Alten Welt* (Zürich, 1965), pp. 867-73.

49 In J. von Arnim, *Stoicorum veterum fragmenta* 3 (Stuttgart, 1964²), pp. 254-57.

50 J. B. Bauer, "Die Ehe bei Musonius und Paulus," *Bibel und Liturgie* 23 (1955-56), pp. 8-13.

51 H. Almquist, *Plutarch und das Neue Testament* (Uppsala, 1946); H. D. Betz, *Plutarch's Theological Writings and Early Christian Literature* (Leiden, 1975); L. Goessler, *Plutarchs Gedanken über die Ehe* (dissertation; Basel, 1962).

52 "You also do I order to remain afar, and let those withdraw from the altar/ whom Venus blessed last night with her joys./ Chastity pleases the gods. Come forward, then, in robes that are pure,/ and with pure hand draw water from the spring."

53 H. Baltensweiler, *Die Ehe im Neuen Testament: Exegetische Untersuchungen über Ehe, Ehelosigkeit und Ehescheidung* (Zürich, 1967). — K. Berger, *Die Gesetzesauslegung Jesu. 1. Markus und Parallelen* (Neukirchen-Vluyn, 1972). — W. Dittmann, *Die Auslegung der Urgeschichte (Genesis Kapitel 1-3) im Neuen Testament* (typed dissertation; Tübingen, 1939). — H. Greeven, "Ehe nach dem Neuen Testament," *New Testament Studies* 15 (1968-69), pp. 365-88. — H. Greeven *et al.*, *Theologie der Ehe* (Göttingen and Regensburg, 1969). — J. Leipoldt, *Die Frau in der antiken Welt und im Urchristentum* (Berlin, 1953 [Leipzig, 1965³], Göttingen, 1962). — K. Niederwimmer, *Askese und Mysterium: Über Ehe, Ehescheidung und Eheverzicht in den Anfängen des christlichen Glaubens* (Göttingen, 1975). — H. Preisker, *Christentum und Ehe in den ersten drei Jahrhunderten* (Berlin, 1927). — B. Reicke, "Neuzeitliche und neutestamentliche Auffassung von Liebe und Ehe," *Novum Testamentum* 1 (1956), pp. 21-34. — K. Rengstorf, *Mann und Frau im Urchristentum* (Cologne-Opladen, 1954).

54 G. Delling, "Ehescheidung," *RAC* 4 (1959). cols. 701-19; J. Dupont, *Mariage et divorce dans l'Evangile: Matthieu 19, 3-12 et par.* (Bruges, 1959); K. Haacker, "Ehescheidung und Wiederverheiratung im Neuen Testament," *Theologische Quartalschrift* 151 (1971), pp. 28-38; P. Hoffman and V. Eid, *Jesus von Nazareth und eine christliche Moral* (Freiburg, 1975), pp. 109-46; B. Schaller, "Die Sprüche über Ehescheidung und Wiederverheiratung in der synoptischen Überlieferung," in E. Lohse *et al.* (eds.), *Der Ruf Jesu und die Antwort der Gemeinde (Festschrift J. Jeremias)* (Göttingen, 1970), pp. 226-46; G. Schneider, "Ehe und Ehescheidung nach dem Neuen Testament," in H. Lubszyk *et al.*, *Ehe unlösbar—Fragen an Bible und Pastoral* (Berlin, 1972), pp. 49-76, 140-47.

55 See my *Theology of the New Testament* 2:25ff.

56 J. Blinzler, "Kind und Königreich Gottes (Mk. 10, 14f)," in his *Aus der Welt und Umwelt des Neuen Testaments: Gesammelte Aufsätze* (Stuttgart, 1969), pp. 41-53; G. Klein, "Jesus und die Kinder," in his *Ärgernisse: Konfrontationen mit dem Neuen Testament* (Munich, 1970), pp. 58-81; S. Légasse, *Jésus et l'enfant* (Paris, 1969).

57 See my *Theology of the New Testament* 3:322-33.

58   Pastoral care and law regarding marriage developed quite
      differently in the Eastern Church than in the Western, al-
      though both started with the New Testament as their source.
      On the basis of Mt. 5:32 and 19:9, the Eastern Church always
      allowed the innocent party in cases of adultery to separate
      and marry again. It also extended this practice to other, quite
      extreme cases. In so doing, it was exercising the "economy"
      or saving function entrusted to it, according to which in cases
      of pastoral need the Church may find solutions that show
      Christ's mercy and take into account the fact of human sin-
      fulness.
           Such teachers of the Eastern Church as Origen, Epi-
      phanius, and Basil gave the reasons for this practice. Latin
      Fathers like Augustine and Ambrosiaster shared their views.
      Even some synods allowed new marriages to guiltless part-
      ners, at least in cases of adultery. Only in the later Middle Ages
      did the strict view win out which forbade divorce or at least
      a new marriage during the lifetime of the former spouse, and
      this no matter what the circumstances. The Council of Trent
      attached its authority to this teaching: Session 24 (November
      11, 1563), canon 7; text in H. Denzinger and A. Schönmetzer,
      Enchiridion symbolorum (32nd ed.; Freiburg, 1963), no. 1807
      (older eds.: no. 977). See B. Bruns, *Ehescheidung und Wieder-*
      heirat im Fall von Ehebruch: Eine rechtsgeschichtliche Unter-
      suchung zu Kanon 7 der 24. Sitzung des Konzils von Trient
      (Munich, 1976); H. Crouzel, *L'Eglise primitive face au di-*
      vorce (Paris, 1971); O. Rousseau, "Divorce and Remarriage:
      East and West," *Concilium*, no. 24 (1967), pp. 113-38. — At
      the Second Vatican Council, Archbishop Elias Zogby, Melkite
      patriarchal vicar for Egypt, made a strong presentation of
      Eastern theology and law on this point; see J. Ch. Hampe,
      Die Autorität der Freiheit 3 (Munich, 1967), pp. 264-69.

59   K. Schäfer, *Zu Gast bei Simon* (Düsseldorf, 1973); H. Schür-
      mann, *Das Lukasevangelium* 1 (Freiburg, 1969), pp. 429-43.

60   U. Becker, *Jesus und due Ehebrecherin: Untersuchungen*
      zur Text- und Überlieferungsgeschichte von Joh 7, 53-8, 11
      (Berlin, 1963); R. Schnackenburg, *Das Johannesevangelium*
      2 (Freiburg, 1975³), pp. 224-36.

61   G. Schneider, "eunouchos," *TDNT* 2:765-68. J. Blinzler,
      "Zur Ehe unfähig . . .': Auslegung von Mt. 19, 12," in his *Aus*

der Welt und Umwelt des Neuen Testaments (n. 56), pp. 20-40, is of the opinion that Jesus was defending himself and the disciples who were unmarried against calumnies. But were the disciples unmarried (1 Cor. 9:5)?

62   Strack-Billerbeck, 1 (1923), p. 891.

63   J. David and F. Schmalz (eds.), *Wie unauflöslich ist die Ehe?* (Aschaffenburg, 1969); H. Harsch (ed.), *Das neue Bild der Ehe* (Munich, 1969); F. Henrich and V. Eid (eds.), *Ehe und Ehescheidung* (Munich, 1972); H. Herrmann, *Ehe und Recht* (Freiburg, 1972); P. J. M. Huizing (ed.), *Für eine neue kirchliche Eheordnung* (Düsseldorf, 1975); H. Lubszyk *et al.*, *Ehe unlösbar—Fragen an Bibel und Pastoral* (Berlin, 1972); V. Steininger, *Auflösbarkeit unauflöslicher Ehen* (Graz, 1968); N. Wetzel (ed.), *Die öffentlichen Sünder, oder: Soll die Kirche Ehen scheiden?* (Mainz, 1970).

64   The distinction between a validly contracted marriage and one that is also consummated by the union of the spouses brings together two originally distinct legal conceptions. According to the one, which is based on ancient Roman law, marriage is founded upon the consent of the partners; according to the other, marriage is definitively contracted through consummation (as medieval law taught). The distinction has some support in Mt. 19:6-7 and Mk. 10:7-8, where it is said that marriage is indissoluble after the spouses have become one. See U. Moseik, *Kirchliches Eherecht unter Berücksichtigung der nachkonziliaren Rechtslage* (Freiburg, 1972²), pp. 268-73.

65   G. Delling, "Ehehindernisse," *RAC* 4 (1959), cols. 862-91.

66   I. Gampel, "Privilegium ut aiunt Petrinum," in W. N. Plöchl and I. Gampel (eds.), *Im Dienst des Rechtes in Kirche und Staat (Festschrift F. Arnold)* (Vienna, 1963), pp. 331-43.

67   According to Catholic teaching, every marriage between baptized Christians is a sacrament. But this principle too raises some serious questions. The Reformers declared marriage to be "something secular." Do Protestant Christians in marrying receive a sacrament without knowing it or wanting it?

68   E. B. Allo, *Première Epître aux Corinthiens* (Paris, 1956²). — H. Conzelmann, *1 Corinthians: A Commentary on the First Epistle to the Corinthians*, tr. J. W. Leitch (Philadelphia,

1975). — H. Lietzmann and W. G. Kümmel, *An die Korinther I/II* (Tübingen, 1969[5]). — D. L. Balch, "Backgrounds of 1 Cor. VII," *New Testament Studies* 18 (1971-72), pp. 351-64. — G. Delling, *Paulus' Stellung zu Frau und Ehe* (Stuttgart, 1931). — A. Feuillet, "La dignité et le rôle de la femme d'après quelques textes pauliniennes," *New Testament Studies* 21 (1974-75), pp. 157-91. — J. M. Ford, "St. Paul, the Philogamist (I Cor. VII), in Early Patristic Exegesis," *New Testament Studies* 11 (1964-65), pp. 326-48. — S. Heine, *Leibhafter Glaube: Ein Bietrag zum Verständnis der theologischen Konzeption des Paulus* (Vienna, 1976). — L. Hick, *Stellung des Heiligen Paulus zur Frau im Rahmen seiner Zeit* (Cologne, 1957). — E. Kähler, *Die Frauen in den paulinischen Briefen* (Zürich-Frankfurt, 1960). — Ch. Maurer, "Ehe und Unzucht nach I Kor. 6, 12-7, 7," *Wort und Dienst* 6 (1959), pp. 159-69. — W. Schrage, "Zur Frontstellung der paulinischen Ehebewertung in I Kor. 7, 1-7," *Zeitschrift für die neutestamentliche Wissenschaft* 67 (1976), pp. 214-34. — I. R. Strieder, *Die Bewertung der Leiblichkeit in den Hauptbriefen des Apostels Paulus* (dissertation; Münster, 1975). — For further literature on Paul and marriage, see also under §5.

69 H. Freier, *Caput velare* (dissertation; Tübingen, 1963), finds that the rite and custom of veiling the head signifies consecration to the divinity. The veil separates the consecrated person or object from society and the world. In particular, it also wards off evil spirits. — A. Jaubert, "La voile des femmes (I Cor. XI, 12-16)," *New Testament Studies* 18 (1971-72), pp. 419-24, gives the interpretation that a woman's veiling with her hair bestows on her the power to pray and prophesy.

70 The German translation issued by commission of the German bishops, *Das Neue Testament* (Stuttgart, 1972), has this note on 1 Cor. 7:1: "This is a citation from the letter the Corinthians had written to Paul" (p. 309).

71 See Strack-Billerbeck, 3 (1926), pp. 372-73.

72 In a sermon of 1519, in *Werke* (Weimar ed.) 2 (1884), p. 168; cited in O. Lähteenmäki, *Sexus und Ehe bei Luther* (Turku, 1955), p. 58.

73 Further material from the rabbinical tradition in Strack-Billerbeck, 3 (1926), pp. 368-71.

74 See Strack-Billerbeck, 3 (1976), p. 372.

75 *Vatican Council II: The Conciliar and Postconciliar Documents*, ed. A. Flannery, O.P. (Collegeville, 1975), pp. 950 and 952.

76 In H. Vorgrimler (ed.), *Commentary on the Documents of Vatican II* 5, tr. W. J. O'Hara (New York, 1969), p. 233.

77 See Strack-Billerbeck, 2 (1924), p. 376, and 4/1 (1928), pp. 378-83.

78 Paul is probably speaking here of fiances about to marry and not of a father who is considering whether or not he should give his daughter in marriage (exegetes have often interpreted the text in this second sense).

79 M. Adinolfi, "La santità del matrimonio in I Thess. 4, 1-8," *Rivista biblica* 24 (1976), pp. 165-84; H. Baltensweiler, "Erwägungen zu I Thess. 4, 3-8," *Theologische Zeitschrift* 19 (1963), pp. 1-13.

80 Commentaries: J. Ernst, *Die Briefe an die Philipper, an Philemon, an die Kolosser, an die Epheser* (Regensburg, 1974), pp. 231-34; E. Lohse, *Colossians and Philemon*, tr. W. R. Poehlmann and R. J. Karris (Philadelphia, 1971), pp. 154-63; E. Schweizer, *Der Brief an die Kolosser* (Zürich and Neukirchen-Vluyn, 1976), pp. 159-71.

   J. E. Crouch, *The Origin and Intention of the Colossian Haustafel* (Göttingen, 1972). Th. Herr, *Naturrecht aus der kritischen Sicht des Neuen Testaments* (Munich, 1976), pp. 34-72: "Die Haustafelethik." E. Kamlah, "*Hypotassesthai* in den neutestamentlichen 'Haustafeln,' " in O. Böcher and K. Haacker (eds.), *Verborum Veritas (Festschrift G. Stählin)* (Wuppertal, 1970), pp. 237-43. W. Schrage, "Zur Ethik der neutestamentlichen Haustafeln," *New Testament Studies* 21 (1974-75), pp. 1-22.

81 Commentaries: J. Gnilka, *Der Epheserbrief* (Freiburg, 1971), pp. 273-94; H. Schlier, *Der Brief an die Epheser* (Düsseldorf, 1968⁶), pp. 252-80; J. Schmid, "Heilige Brautschaft," *RAC* 2 (1954), cols. 528-64; A. R. Batey, *New Testament Nuptial Imagery* (Leiden, 1931); K. M. Fischer, *Tendenz und Absicht des Epheserbriefes* (Göttingen, 1973), pp. 79-147, 176-200.

82 On the Church as body of Christ, see my *Theology of the New Testament* 4:29-32.

83 E. Christen, "Ehe als Sakrament: Neue Gesichtspunkte aus

Exegese und Dogmatik." *Theologische Berichte* 1 (Zürich, 1972), pp. 11-68; J. Duss-von Werdt, "Theologie der Ehe: Der sakramentale Charakter der Ehe," in J. Feiner and M. Löhrer (eds.), *Mysterium salutis* 4/2 (Einsiedeln, 1973), pp. 422-49; K. Rahner, "Marriage as a Sacrament," in his *Theological Investigations* 10, tr. D. Bourke (New York, 1973), pp. 199-221.

84 See my *Theology of the New Testament* 4:118-22.

85 N. Brox, *Die Pastoralbriefe* (Regensburg, 1969), pp. 185-87: "Der Witwenstand"; C. Spicq, *Les épîtres pastorales* 1 (Paris, 1969⁴), pp. 385-425: "La femme chrétienne et ses vertus"; U. B. Müller, *Zur frühchristlichen Theologiegeschichte: Judenchristentum und Paulinismus in Kleinasien am Wende vom. 1. zum 2. Jahrh. n. Chr.* (Gütersloh, 1976), pp. 53-77: "Der geschichtliche Ort der Gegner in den Pastoralbriefen."

86 The commandment and ideal of "one marriage" seem to mean different things in 1 Tim. 3:2 and 1 Tim. 5:9. 1 Tim. 3:2, as viewed in the light of contemporary catalogues of vices, requires that a bishop be not involved in a relationship with any woman but his wife. According to 1 Tim. 5:9, the ideal is that a widow have been married only once, just as the virtue of the wife who has been married only once is praised in literary texts and inscriptions. In other words, the popular moral outlook made different demands on husband and wife.

　　See B. Kötting and Th. Hopfner, "Bigamie," *RAC* 2 (1954), cols. 282-86; B. Kötting, "Bigamus," *RAC* 3 (1957), cols. 1016-24; H. Funke, "Univira," *Jahrbuch für Antike und Christentum* 8-9 (1965-66), pp. 183-88; B. Kötting, " 'Univira' in Inschriften," in W. den Boer *et al.* (eds.), *Romanitas et Christianitas (Festschrift J. H. Waszink)* (Amsterdam, 1973), pp. 195-206 (*univira*—"wife to a single husband"—can either be a term of praise for fidelity in marriage or a term of esteem for a woman married only once); P. Trummer, "Einehe nach den Pastoralbriefen," *Biblica* 51 (1970), pp. 471-84.

87 G. Stählin, "chēra," *TDNT* 9:440-65; "Das Bild der Witwe," *Jahrbuch für Antike und Christentum* 17 (1974), pp. 5-20.

88 Of interest is the regulation of clothing in a first-century inscription for a shrine in Andania (Peleponnesus). Text in W. Dittenberger, *Sylloge Inscriptionum Graecarum* 2 (Hildescheim, 1960⁴), p. 403, no. 736, IV: "The women who serve in

the mysteries may not wear any golden ornaments; they are not to use either rouge or ceruse or wear a circlet in their hair or braid their hair, or wear shoes made of felt or of the skins of sacrificial animals."

89 W. Weicht, *Die dem Lamme folgen: Eine Untersuchung der Auslegung von Offb 14, 1-5 in den letzten achtzig Jahren* (dissertation, Gregorian University, Rome; Untermerzbach-Bamberg, 1976); this author takes *parthenoi* in a figurative sense. H. Kraft, *Die Offenbarung des Johannes* (Tübingen, 1974), pp. 189-91, gives a different explanation. The original text of 14:4, according to Kraft, was simply: "It is these who have not defiled themselves with women"; that is, it was said of the 144,000 redeemed that they had avoided unchastity. This was consonant with the fact that the literature of early Judaism contained urgent warnings against immorality (§§2.4 and 2.5). The text then went on to say in 14:5 that the blessed had also avoided lying (in accordance with the frequent urging of Scripture; e.g., Ps. 32:2; Is. 53:9; Zeph. 3:13). The words "for they are virgins" (i.e., celibates) were later added to the clause "who have not defiled themselves with women." This addition came from a time of excessive asceticism in the Church; they show a misunderstanding of the original text and distort its meaning.

90 "Frau," *RAC* 8 (1972), cols. 265-66.

91 F. Kullien, G. Binder, and L. Kötsche-Breitenbruch, "Geburt," *RAC* 9 (1976), cols. 36-216.

92 H. Braun, *Qumran und das Neue Testament* 1 (Tübingen, 1966), pp. 213-18.

93 See my *Theology of the New Testament* 4:132.

94 H. Deichgräber, *Der Hippocratische Eid* (Stuttgart, 1953). P. Sardi, *L'aborto ieri e oggi* (Briescia, 1975).

95 The Septuagint (LXX) has *paidion mē exeikonismenon*. The word *exeikonismenon* is very rare and apparently was not used prior to the LXX. Is the LXX picking up the words of Gen. 1:26: "Let us make man after our image (*kat'eikona hēmeteran*)"? If it is, then it is saying that the developed embryo has the form of God.

96 H. Waszink, "Abtreibung," *RAC* 1 (1950), cols. 55-60; F. J. Dölger, "Das Lebensrecht des ungeborenen Kindes and die Fruchtabtreibung in der heidnischen und christlichen Antike,"

in his *Antike und Christentum* 4 (1934), pp. 1-61.

97 M. Lidzbarski, *Rechtes Ginza* (Göttingen-Leipzig, 1925), p. 185.

98 J. Baumann (ed.), *Das Abtreibungsverbot des §218 StGB: Eine Vorschrift, die mehr schadet als nützt* (Neuwied-Berlin, 1972); P. Eicher, *Solidarischer Glaube* (Düsseldorf, 1975), pp. 110-35: "Für einen Humanismus ab ovo"; J. Grundel (ed.), Abtreibung pro und contra (Innsbruck, 1971); B. Häring, *The Law of Christ*, tr. E. G. Kaiser, 3 (Westminster, Md., 1966), pp. 205-13; K. Hörmann, *Lexikon der christlichen Moral* (Innsbruck, 1976²), pp. 3-17; J. G. Ziegler, "Abtreibung," in J. B. Bauer (ed.), *Die heissen Eisen von A bis Z* (Graz, 1972), pp. 13-16.

99 Text in H. Denzinger and A. Schönmetzer, *Enchiridion symbolorum* (35th ed.; Freiburg, 1974), nos. 3258 and 3298.

100 *Ibid.*, no. 3720.

101 *Pio XII, Discorsi e radiomessaggi* 13 (1951-52), pp. 331-53 and 413-18.

102 *The Pope Speaks* 21 (1976), pp. 60-73.

103 G. Heinzelmann *et al.*, *Wir schweigen nicht länger* (Zürich, n.d.); *Die getrennten Schwestern* (Zürich, 1967). The following periodicals discuss our theme in approximately simultaneous issues: *Concilium* (German ed.) 12 (1976), no. 1; *Theological Studies* 36 (1975), no. 4; *Theologische Quartalschrift* 156 (1976), no. 2.

104 W. Garrison, *Women in the Life of Jesus* (Indianapolis, 1962). For further literature, see §7.

105 *Commentaria in Evangelium Ioannis* 13, 28 (*PG* 14:448B) and 13, 29 (*PG* 14:449D).

106 *Commentaria in Evangelium Ioannis* 4, 28ff. (*PG* 123:1241D).

107 *Commentaria in Cantica Canticorum* 3, 1-4 (*GCS* 1/1:354).

108 *Sermo* 132, 1, ed. A. Mai, *Nova Patrum Biblioteca* 1 (Rome, 1852).

109 *Sermones in Cantica Canticorum* 75, 8 (*PL* 183:1148B).

110 O. Michel, "oikos," *TDNT* 5:119-34; E. Schweizer, *Der Brief an die Kolosser* (Zürich and Neukirchen-Vluyn, 1976), pp. 176-77; P. Stuhlmacher, *Der Brief an Philemon* (Zürich and Neukirchen-Vluyn, 1975), pp. 70-75.

111 A. Kalsbach, "Diakonisse, *RAC* 3 (1957), cols. 917-28; J. Funk, "*Klerikale* Frauen?" *Österreichisches Archiv für Kirchenrecht* 14 (1963), pp. 271-90; R. Gryson, *The Ministry of Women in the Early Church* (Collegeville, Minn., 1976), pp. 30ff.

It would really be misleading for the contemporary German to call her a deaconess, since this name is applied to nurses. [A *Diakonissin* is a Lutheran nurse. In England and America, too, a "deaconess" is a church worker, and especially one belonging to an order or sisterhood and consecrated to a life of service. This, however, has not prevented British (JB, Philips) and American (RSV, NAB) translators from calling Phoebe a "deaconess." This is the term we shall use henceforth in the text. — Tr.]

112 In the earliest days of the Church, men and women alike were called "deacons." The term "deaconess" appears first in Canon 19 of the Council of·Nicaea.

113 See my *Theology of the New Testament* 4:84-85.

114 R. Freudenberger, *Das Verhalten der römischen Behörden gegen die Christen im 2. Jahrhundert* (Munich, 1965), pp. 17-18.

115 H. Krämer, K. H. Rendtorff, R. Meyer, and G. Friedrich, "prophētes," *TDNT* 6:781-861; G. Dautzenberg, *Urchristliche Prophetie: Ihre Erforschung, ihre Voraussetzung im Judentum and ihre Struktur im ersten Korintherbrief* (Stuttgart, 1975); U. B. Müller, *Prophetie und Predigt im Neuen Testament* (Gütersloh, 1975).

116 See my *Theology of the New Testament* 4:75-77.

117 G. Fitzer, "*Das Weib schweige in der Gemeinde*": *Über dem unpaulinischen Charakter der mulier-taceat Verse in I Korinther 14* (Munich, 1963). — The question is usually discussed in the literature mentioned in §6, as well as in commentaries on First Corinthians.

118 G. G. Blum, "Das Amt der Frau im Neuen Testament," *Novum Testamentum* 7 (1963), pp. 142-61. — M. Daly, *The Church and the Second Sex* (New York, 1968). — J. Daniélou, *The Ministry of Women in the Early Church* (London, 1961). — E. C. Ewitt and S. R. Hiatt, *Women Priests?* (New York, 1973). — A. Feuillet, *Jésus et sa mère: Le rôle de la Vierge*

Marie dans l'histoire du salut et la place de la femme dans l'Eglise (Paris, 1974). — J. M. Ford, "Biblical Material Relevant to the Ordination of Women," *Journal of Ecumenical Studies* 10 (1973), pp. 669-99. — J. Funk, "Klerikale Frauen?" *Österreichisches Archiv für Kirchenrecht* 14 (1963), pp. 271-90. — R. Gallay, *Des femmes prêtres?* (Paris, 1973). — J. Galot, *Mission et ministère de la femme* (Paris, 1973). — P. Jordan, "Frauen ante portas?" *Schweizerische Kirchenzeitung* 44 (1976), pp. 641-45. — H. van der Meer, *Women Priests in the Catholic Church*, tr. A. and L. Swidler (Philadelphia, 1973). — J. Th. Münch, "Katholische Priesterinnen?" *Der christliche Sonntag* 41 (1965), pp. 641-45. — K. Rahner, "Priestertum der Frau?" *Stimmen der Zeit* 102 (1977), pp. 291-301. — I. Raming, *Der Ausschluss der Frau vom priesterlichen Amt—gottgewollte Tradition oder Diskriminierung?* (Cologne, 1973). — H. Wilson, *Women Priests?* (Surrey, 1975).

119 Translated in Flannery (ed.), *Vatican Council II: The Conciliar and Postconciliar Documents*, p. 389.

120 *Ibid.*, p. 929. See also no. 60.

121 *Ibid.*, p. 777.

122 [The newspaper article is citing the address of Pope Paul VI on Women in the Life of Society, to the Congress of the Italian Women's Center (December 6, 1976), tr. in *The Pope Speaks* 22 (1977), pp. 22-25.

123 See my *Theology of the New Testament* 4:67-73.

124 *The Ordination of Women*, tr. in *The Pope Speaks* 22 (1977), pp. 108-22. The quotations in the text are from this translation.

125 *Gemeinsame Synode der Bistümer in der Bunderepublik Deutschland* (Freiburg, 1976²), pp. 611-12, 616-17.

RAC   *Reallexikon für Antike und Christentum.*
              Stuttgart, 1941 (1950)-

TDNT   *Theological Dictionary of the New Testa-*
              ment. Grand Rapids, 1964-74

CSEL   *Corpus Scriptorum Ecclesiasticorum Lat-*
              inorum. Vienna, 1866-

PL   *Patrologia Latina,* ed. J. P. Migne. Paris,
              1844-64

CCL   *Corpus Christianorum, Series Latina.* Turn-
              hout, 1953-

GCS   *Die griechischen christlichen Schriftsteller*
              der ersten drei Jahrhunderte. Leipzig, 1897-
              1941; Berlin and Leipzig, 1953; Berlin, 1954-